ADVENTUROUS PUB WALKS IN WORCESTERSHIRE

Roy Woodcock

COUNTRYSIDE BOOKS
NEWBURY BERKSHIRE

First published 2006

COUNTRYSIDE BOOKS
3 Catherine Road
Newbury, Berkshire

To view our complete range of books,
please visit us at
www.countrysidebooks.co.uk

ISBN 1 85306 889 6
EAN 978 1 85306 889 8

Designed by Peter Davies, Nautilus Design
Cover picture of the Malvern Hills by Derek Forss
Photographs by the author

Produced through MRM Associates Ltd., Reading
Typeset by Techniset Typesetters, Newton-le-Willows
Printed by Woolnough Bookbinding Ltd., Irthlingborough

CONTENTS

AREA MAP SHOWING THE LOCATION OF THE WALKS

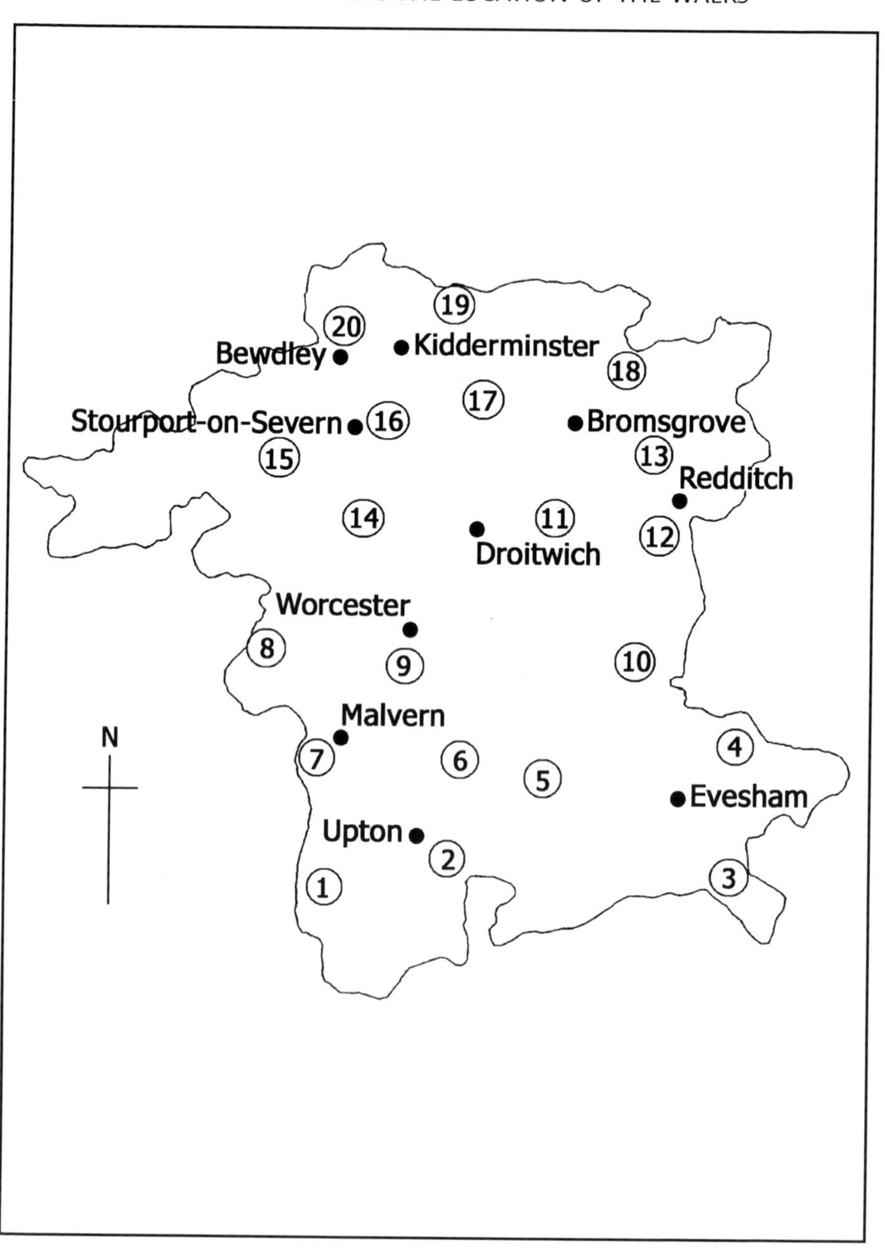

INTRODUCTION

Worcestershire is a beautiful county and selecting locations for 20 walks is inevitably subjective. But I have known the county since childhood, and it has been fun finding new places to walk, as well as revisiting old haunts – 40 years later. There are miles of delightful countryside, well provided with footpaths, which attracts large numbers of walkers.

Fine views can be had from the Malvern Hills and their northerly extensions, the Abberleys, in the south-west of the county, as well as from the Lickeys and Clent in the north. These have been created by the old hard rocks which have resisted erosion for hundreds of millions of years.

Much of the county is made up of lowland river valleys. The Severn crosses through the middle of the county from north to south and is joined by its two main tributaries, the Teme and the Avon. These provide idyllic walks in spring, summer and autumn, though flooding can sometimes be a nuisance in the winter months.

THE CANAL BASIN AT STOURPORT.

Amongst the attractions to be visited on these walks are hill forts, battlefield sites, the largest set of locks on any canal in the country, ancient woodlands such as Wyre Forest or Chaddesley Woods, and several nature reserves and sites managed by Worcestershire Wildlife Trust.

Each route is accompanied by a sketch map, although it is sensible to carry the relevant OS map in your rucksack as well. The walks range from 7½ to 10¾ miles in length and all have a pub located somewhere along the route, and there are often suitable picnic places, which are mentioned at relevant stages in the directions.

We all hope for fine weather, which makes walking more comfortable and enjoyable, but it cannot always be guaranteed and it is recommended therefore that you wear appropriate clothing. Long trousers are often preferable to shorts in the summer, as vegetation begins to spread onto footpaths. It is also a good idea to take waterproofs if rain is forecast, and to carry a cool drink in hot weather and a small flask of tea or coffee in cold weather. One thing you can be sure of though is that you will never be very far from a pub or a shop if refreshment is required, and all those I have mentioned in this book will be able to provide you with a good meal – pub grub at its best! Good walking!

Roy Woodcock

PUBLISHER'S NOTE

We hope that you obtain considerable enjoyment from this book; great care has been taken in its preparation. Although at the time of publication all routes followed public rights of way or permitted paths, diversion orders can be made and permissions withdrawn.

We cannot, of course, be held responsible for such diversion orders and any inaccuracies in the text which result from these or any other changes to the routes nor any damage which might result from walkers trespassing on private property. We are anxious though that all details covering the walks are kept up to date and would therefore welcome information from readers which would be relevant to future editions.

The simple sketch maps that accompany the walks in this book are based on notes made by the author whilst checking out the routes on the ground. However, for the benefit of a proper map, we do recommend that you purchase the relevant Ordnance Survey sheet covering your walk. The Ordnance Survey maps are widely available, especially through booksellers and local newsagents.

Walk 1

CASTLEMORTON COMMON TO HEREFORDSHIRE BEACON

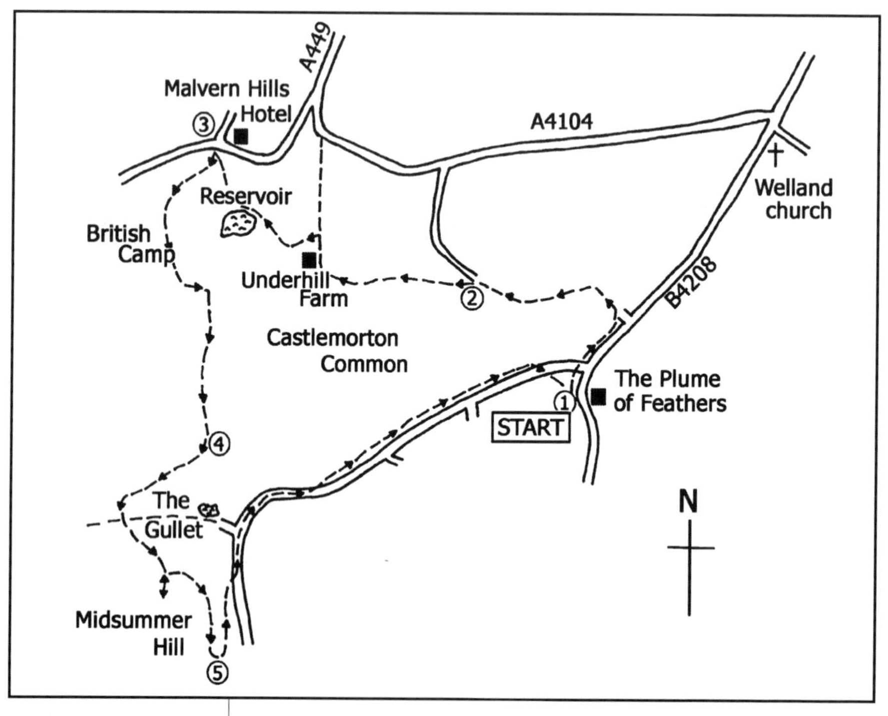

Distance:
9½ miles

Starting point:
The Plume of Feathers car park, with permission. GR 787388

Map: OS Explorer 190 Malvern Hills and Bredon Hill

How to get there: *From Upton take the A4104 to Welland. Turn left along the B4208 for nearly a mile and the pub is on the left-hand side. From Malvern take the A449 southwards towards Malvern Wells and Little Malvern. Fork left at Little Malvern along the A4104 signed to Upton, and then turn right at Welland along the B4208. Parking places are available at the pub with permission, or alongside the common between Welland and the pub.*

UNDERHILL FARM, WITH A VIEW OF HEREFORDSHIRE BEACON.

No book of walks on Worcestershire would be complete without a visit to the Malvern Hills, one of Britain's most distinctive landscape features. Here we visit the southern half of the hills, walking across the common and climbing up to the Iron Age fort on top of the Herefordshire Beacon. We then turn south along the ridge top, from the very busy area around the British Camp, to the quieter Swinyard and Midsummer hills to visit a second Iron Age fort before descending to the common again.

The Plume of Feathers is wonderfully situated on the edge of Castlemorton Common. This freehouse is open all day and welcomes walkers, as well as dogs and children. The small bar is the oldest part of the pub, dating from the 16th century, with a slightly later restaurant area. There is ample parking space at the front, where tables and umbrellas provide a sitting out area for hot summer days.

Hobson and Goff's *are popular beers available, as well as Stowford cider – all from fairly local producers. Sandwiches and full meals are available daily. Telephone 01684 833554.*

① Cross the road from the pub and turn right. Ignore the left turn signed to **Swinyard** car park and follow the edge of the common, with Welland church spire straight ahead – though we are not going so far. Once past the houses on the right there is open common on both sides, and after a further 400 yards reach a narrow surfaced road. Turn left here and follow this road, as it wanders across the common, bridging a small stream lined with willows. The narrow road bends left, and we proceed along the edge of the common. Pass a few houses, including Strawbyn Kennels and Cattery, and eventually reach a gate across the road. (1½ miles)

② At this point leave the road, by going left over a plank footbridge, and then follow a stony track close to the hedge on our right. The track leads us to the end of the common, and we keep ahead, on the broad grassy track between hedges and fields. Climbing slightly we reach a small wooden gate where two footpaths are signed. Keep right here, with a fence and hedge on our right, heading towards the black and white **Underhills Farm**. At the end of this field, go through a large metal gate and along the track to pass in front of the farm buildings. Follow the concrete track and, at the top of the slight rise, the tower of **Little Malvern Priory church** comes into view. On the left by a coniferous tree is a gate and stile, where we turn. Head straight across this small field to a large gate, and into the woods. Follow the narrow path, rocky in places, climbing through the woods. A stream flows alongside the path and at a major path we turn right, soon to emerge from the woods, with the stream on the left.

Climbing steadily, along the track created with concrete blocks which allow greenery to grow in between, we pass the reservoir on the left. Ahead is the steep slope of the **Herefordshire Beacon**, the only location where heather grows on the Malvern Hills. Soon reach a large car park, opposite the **Malvern Hills Hotel**. (1¾ miles)

Created in 1884 by the Malvern Hills Act, which aimed to prevent further enclosure of what had been common land, the Malvern Hills Conservators are one of the

world's oldest organisations concerned with conservation. They manage nearly 300 acres of which half is hill land, and the remainder commons or verges. Some of the Conservators are elected by local residents and the remainder are appointed by local authorities. Their duties include preventing encroachment onto the commons, and keeping the hills and commons open for everyone to enjoy. Control of vegetation as well as erosion are major on-going problems. Local residents provide two-thirds of the funding and the remainder comes from charging car parking fees, and grants from the County Council, English Nature and the Countryside Agency.

③ From the car park, pass the Conservators' notice and take the track signed to the Herefordshire Beacon, generally known as **British Camp**, which reaches a height of 1,115 ft (340 m). This very popular route has been surfaced to prevent footpath erosion. From the summit, all-round views are quite stunning, into Wales, or across to the Cotswolds, or south to the obelisk and May Hill.

Parts of the earthworks date from as long ago as the 4th century BC though more work was completed on ditches and embankments in the 3rd and 2nd centuries BC. One of the finest hill forts in Britain, the embankments enclose an area of twelve hectares (30 acres) occupied by up to 2,000 inhabitants. The camp is thought to have been in use until Roman times, and then again by the Normans in the 12th century.

Walk southwards along the ridge towards the southern gateway, and descend the stony path (designed to reduce erosion) to a round marker stone, where we turn right. The path leads us past the small cave known as **Giant's** or **Clutter's**, cut out of very hard basalt. Descend to a

THE PLUME OF FEATHERS.

hollow called **Silurian Pass**, indicating a change in the geology. Several paths meet here, but keep ahead and climb on to the next part of the ridge, which is **Swinyard Hill**. **Castlemorton Common** opens out to the left, with the hills and woods of Herefordshire to the right. **Eastnor Park** extends to the right and in this estate can be seen the castle (built 1812-15), and the obelisk. Built of Cotswold limestone in 1812 by the first Lord Somers, the obelisk is a memorial to his son who had died that year in the Peninsular War. (1¾ miles)

Castlemorton Common was formerly part of Malvern Chase, originally created as royal hunting grounds in medieval times and then handed over by the king to local noblemen such as Gilbert de Clare, Earl of Gloucester. The common is managed by the Malvern Hills Conservators, having been bought in 1962 and 1966 (from the Church Commissioners). The unenclosed area of scrub and grassland is being maintained as a common though more trees and scrub exist nowadays than formerly. But there are still sheep and some cattle now, and Conservators clear scrub by cutting or burning, in order to maintain a suitable habitat for a range of wildlife, as well as public enjoyment. Part is designated as a Site of Special Scientific Interest. In spite of its name, common land is not available for anyone or everyone to use for grazing animals, but it is an area with real freedom to roam.

④ At the round marker stone before reaching the top of a huge quarry, turn right following the sign to **Midsummer Hill** and the obelisk and descend slightly into the woods. Turn left along the broad track which can be very muddy after wet weather. Reach a cross path, where the right turn is the path into **Eastnor Park** and the left turn is to the **Gullet**. Keep straight ahead, along the stony track. Rising steadily, once past the small windmill and the house down to the left, turn left to follow the narrow path alongside the hedge and fence. This leads up to the National Trust Midsummer Hill sign by the first of the embankments of the old Iron Age fort. Here is the North Gate of the Midsummer Hill encampment. Just beyond the outermost embankment of this Iron Age fort, the path to the left is our onward route, but first keep ahead to visit the top of the hill. At the summit (932 ft/284 m) is a concrete and stone shelter containing a plaque stating that the Iron Age hill fort was given to the National Trust in 1923, in memory of Captain Reginald Somers Cocks M.C. from Eastnor.

Retrace your steps and just before reaching the outer limit of the fort, go right, along a clear path heading into the woods through the bracken. This path descends steadily, and then rises slightly before emerging on to **Hollybush Hill**, and the location of the main section of the fort. Turn right here to walk along the open grassy area.

The fort encloses about 20 acres/ 8 ha. Excavations took place in 1965-70 and evidence was found of at least 200 buildings. Several of the low banks and mounds are remnants of medieval cultivation and the low rectangular pillow mound was probably a medieval rabbit warren. Note the numerous anthills – yellow meadow ants – popular with green woodpeckers.

As we approach the southern end of the grassy area, the old embankments can be seen on the left, and across to our right the rock at the top of the large quarry comes into view. (2 miles)

⑤ Turn sharp left at the end of the grassy area, to go over the embankment and leave the site of the fort. The path crosses a ditch and then another embankment before descending steadily through the woods, to follow a clear path from **Hollybush Hill** down to the road. Just before reaching the road, note the path joining us from the left (signed steep route to **Midsummer Hill** – beginning with a few steps). Turn left along the narrow road, forking right when it divides, and descend slightly before climbing a little to reach the edge of **Castlemorton Common**. Pass the new parking area and walk alongside the common.

A gentle stroll of just over a mile takes us back to the **Plume of Feathers**, passing a pond on the left, with a population of newts, and a small group of the rare black poplars. Sheep or cattle are likely to be grazing around here. There will certainly be interesting bird life, especially in summer when visiting warblers have arrived. At other times of the year, stonechats, pipits and yellowhammers can be seen, as well as snipe in the damper patches. (2½ miles)

Date walk completed:

UPTON UPON SEVERN TO RIPPLE

THE GRAVEL WORKINGS THAT ARE CHANGING THE COUNTRYSIDE – IF ONLY TEMPORARILY.

Distance:
8½ miles

Starting point:
The pay and display car park in Upton upon Severn. GR 850407

Maps: OS Explorer 190 Malvern Hills and Bredon Hill or Landranger 150 Worcester and The Malverns

How to get there: *The starting point is at the car park 50 yards north of the bridge across the Severn. This point can be reached by the A38 Worcester to Tewkesbury road, turning along the A4104 to reach Upton upon Severn. Upton can also be reached from Malvern, along the B4211 or the A449 and the A4104. There is also a free car park at the far end of the village, opposite the church.*

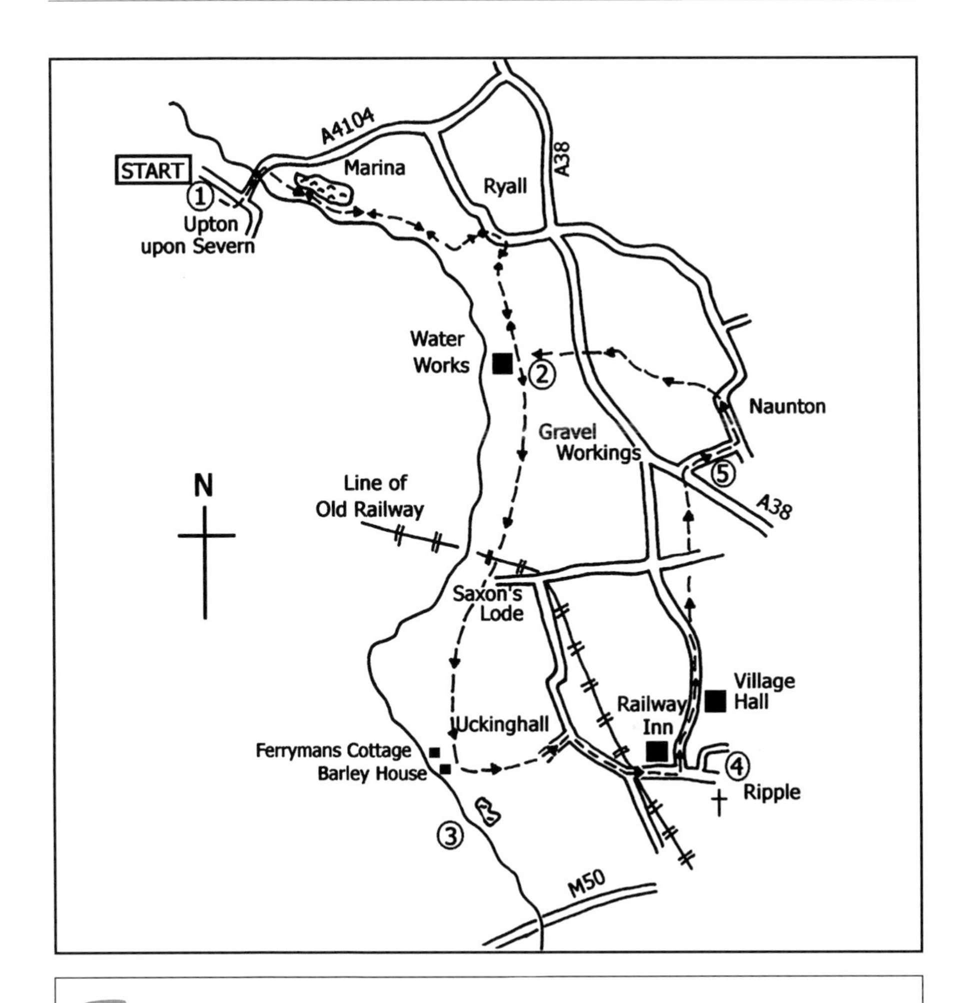

The walk begins in the attractive riverside town of Upton upon Severn and passes through the small settlements of Ryall, Ripple, Uckinghall and Naunton – the last of which achieved unaccustomed fame as the home of Leslie Law, Olympic Equestrian gold medal winner in 2004. Gentle undulating countryside and delightful willow-lined river banks are part of this walk, as well as gravel workings which are temporarily changing the countryside – although all will be restored. The flooded gravel pits are major attractions for wildlife, especially a variety of birds feeding or nesting here.

The Railway Inn at Ripple is well known for its fine ales. It is used by locals, as well as walkers and anglers – and horse riders too, taking advantage of the hitching pole near the drinking trough at the roadside. The restaurant is situated at the front of the pub, with a function room and skittle alley to the rear and a large car park, too.

It is open for food *from Tuesday to Sunday lunchtimes, and offers home-cooked food, with a good choice. Especially popular with regulars and locals, and guaranteed to satisfy the most hungry of walkers, is the Sunday lunch – noted for quality, price and quantity.*
Telephone: 01684 592225.

The Walk

① From the car park in **Upton** walk along the road to the river bridge close to the **Pepperpot**, the tower of the former medieval church and now a Heritage Centre. Once across the bridge (a scene of action in the Civil War in 1651), turn right along the narrow road, following a footpath sign for the **Severn Way**. Pass a house on the right and reach another narrow road. Go left here for 20 yards and then turn right, with riverside houses on the right. The marina is soon reached on the left. Cross over the high footbridge and follow a broad track through trees to a small gate and keep ahead along the edge of the large field. The river is to the right and a small embankment is on the left. A few houses have been built at the top of the valley margin to our left, with good views across the riverside meadows, called the hams, which occasionally are flooded in winter.

At the end of the large field, move slightly left away from the river along a broad path with a fence on the right and narrow woodland on the slope to the left. At the top of this ascent, the path divides and we turn right for a few yards to reach a road. Turn left here and follow the road between modern houses to reach a major road. Turn right here and after about 30 yards, as the road bends left, we turn right. There are two right turns and we take the second of these, not Ryall Lane.

Walk on passing the old farm on our left, now modernised, to reach a large gate with a stile alongside. Go over here and keep straight ahead along the field margin, and through (or over) an old gate. Pass a large barn on the right, and soon reach a footpath going left, and then a driveway, which is the route of the return walk after we have been to **Ripple**. (1 1/2 miles)

We are now in the territory of the gravel company – an industrial site in a very rural area. The gravels were probably deposited by an enlarged River Severn carrying melt water and rocks during the Ice Age. When gravel extraction is terminated, the landscape will be restored and probably will become a nature reserve.

② Keep straight ahead across the driveway which links the Severn Trent Water Works and quarry buildings with the main A38 road away to our left. Follow the clearly signed and fenced footpath through the gravel workings. Beware of the trucks which may be rushing around in this area. The route of the footpath is clearly shown but is not the same as shown on the OS map! Just follow this path, admiring the views to the **Malverns** on the right.

At the end of the quarry workings is a hollow and small lake, where sand martins nest – a 'Keep Out' notice may locate this spot for you as you walk past. The entire digging area is becoming a remarkable nature reserve, with badgers, foxes, many birds and wildflowers.

As we approach the buildings of Saxon's Lode, probably named after the Sexton family and not

THE RAILWAY INN AT RIPPLE.

the early Anglo-Saxons, notice across the river the embankment on which the old railway line from Malvern to Upton and Tewkesbury ran. Away to our left is an iron fence and old building, a relic of an oil storage depot from the times when oil tankers came up the River Severn.

Keep straight ahead towards the farm, passing a bungalow on the right and then **Saxon's Lode Cottage**, and walk into the farmyard. As the farm drive bends to the left, an arrow and a stile point the way straight ahead near the right margin of a field, with the pond just on our right. Cross a long narrow field to a white-tipped post and stile in the far right corner. Continue across the middle of the next field to a double stile by a gnarled old tree, with a bunch of mistletoe overhead at the stile. Cross another field to a double stile and footbridge. The traffic on the M50 will be clearly visible ahead, as we cross the next very large field towards the houses on the riverbank. (1½ miles)

This field is Uckinghall Meadow which has links with Ripple church. In the churchyard is the grave of the Ripple Giant, Robert Reeve, who died in 1626 after mowing this large 100-acre meadow in a day, for a wager.

③ When we reach the embankment close to the two modern houses, **Barley House** and **Ferrymans Cottage**, there is a path continuing along the riverbank, passing the site of the former ferry. Turn left just before the two houses and follow the drive towards the village of **Uckinghall**. On our right we pass the entrance to **Ripple Fisheries**, used by Birmingham Angling Association. The track soon becomes a narrow surfaced road, lined with ditches, willow trees, occasional flood marker posts, and several houses with attractive gardens. Look out for the gardens with old cider presses. At a T-junction with a small triangle of grass, turn right and climb a slight hill to reach the old railway bridge where the sign points to Ripple. Continue on across here to reach the **Railway Inn**. Pause for refreshment if required, and then continue straight ahead. The onward walk takes the first turn left, signed to Severn Stoke and Worcester, but first go on ahead past the small village green, with its 14th-century preaching cross and visit the remarkable late 12th-century church of St Mary. (1¼ miles)

The liassic stone church is particularly famous for its 15th-century misericords, twelve of which depict the labours of the seasons. Ripple is an older settlement than Upton and was the site of a battle in the Civil War, in 1643.

④ Retrace your steps from the church to the second turning (**School Lane**), the road signed to **Severn Stoke**, and turn right here. Walk between houses and leave the village to reach the village hall on the right. Shortly beyond here pass a large barn a few yards to the right, where we leave the road over a stile heading diagonally across a large field. Pass just to the right of the buildings which protrude into this field and head towards two large brown buildings. Reach a stile and a narrow road, and keep straight ahead over another stile to the left of the large buildings of the Large Animal and Equine Surgery. Stay close to the hedge and pass over another stile, with great views to the full length of the **Malvern** ridge on our left and **Bredon Hill** to the right. Walk straight ahead, with small fenced paddocks to the right, to reach a stile and the main A38 road. (1¼ miles)

⑤ Cross straight over and continue along the narrow road signed to **Naunton**, and after 300 yards it bends left. A further 250 yards on it bends right, and at this point, with a black and white house straight in front, turn left along a short track which leads into a field. Go diagonally right across to the far corner of this field and along the left side of the hedge bordering the next field. Half way along this hedge go right, over a stile and then diagonally across the next field aiming towards a gap in the hedge, just to the left of the line looking towards a lone house. Stay close to the hedge on the left, with the lone house across the field to the right, and reach a step stile and the main A38 road again. Cross straight over to a stile leading into the gravel workings. Follow the track for about 300 yards to reach a T-junction of paths and tracks. (1½ miles)

⑥ We are now back at point number 2, and we turn right to retrace our steps back to the road in **Ryall**. Turn left for about 30 yards then left along **Ryall Meadow** to reach the path which leads back to **Upton** and the starting point. (1½ miles)

Date walk completed:

Walk 3

BROADWAY AND BUCKLAND

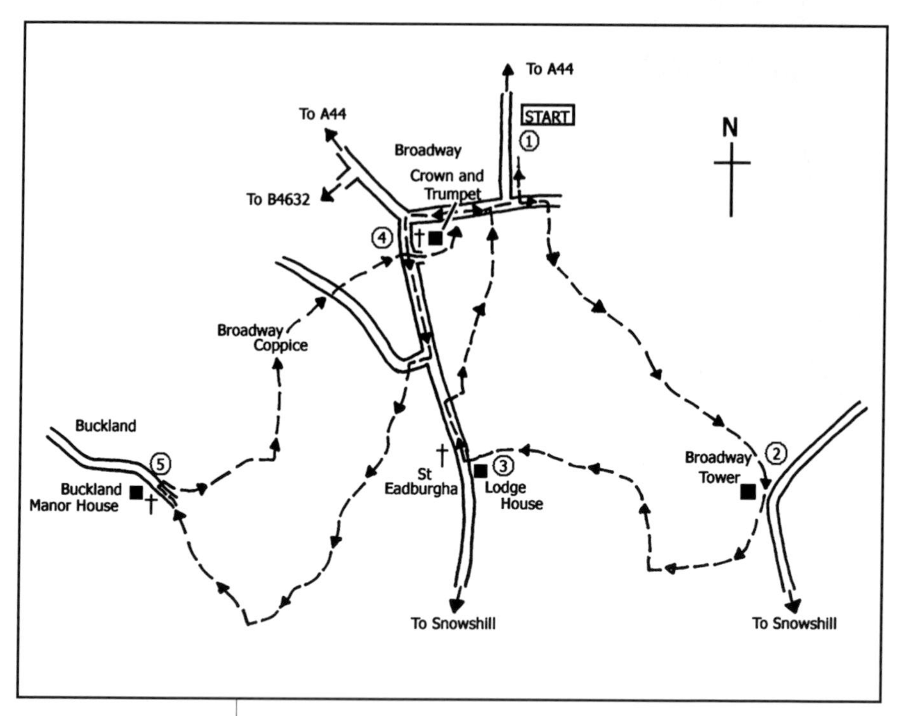

Distance:
9¼ miles

Starting point:
The car park on Leamington Road in Broadway.
GR 100377

Maps: OS Landranger 150 Worcester and the Malverns and Explorer OL45 The Cotswolds

How to get there: *Broadway is reached along the A44 from Evesham or from Chipping Norton. Turn into the village along the B4632 Willersley to Broadway road, and this leads directly to the car park on Leamington Road.*

THE GATEHOUSE OF BROADWAY COURT.

Arguably the most famous and certainly one of the most attractive of the Cotswold villages, Broadway stands at the foot of the Cotswold scarp. Built of local mellow yellowish limestone, the main street is extremely photogenic and a honeypot for tourists, at all times of the year. It may be difficult to leave such an attractive village, but the countryside all around will tempt anyone. Green fields, woods and hedges, birds, flowers and butterflies, as well as stone walls and picturesque buildings will delight all comers to this beautiful part of England. We walk in two circuits from Broadway, firstly up to the Broadway Tower and Country Park and then, after refreshment in the village, a second circuit takes us to the neighbouring small village of Buckland.

The Crown and Trumpet is situated on Church Street, between the village green and the church. This stone-built, 17th-century pub is open all day, but with shorter hours in the winter. Oak beams and a log fire are attractive features. Many pub games are available, not only darts and dominoes, but also the unusual Devil among the Tailors, Shut the Box and the unique Ring the Bull.

It offers a wide choice *of good food and a selection of beers, including Old Hooky, Old Speckled Hen and Cotterswold Gold from the Stanton brewery. Telephone: 01386 853202.*

① Leave the car park on **Leamington Road**, and walk along the path behind the toilet block. This leads through to the main road in the village. Turn left here and notice the old milestone (London 90 miles) by the **Milestone House.** Cross over the road to turn right, following the sign to **The Cotswold Way** and **Fish Hill Picnic Place**.

Walk along the drive, through a wooden gate and a small metal kissing gate, then along the left side of the field. Cross over a small stream and begin to climb, up to another kissing gate. Turn slightly left and head up the middle of the field through remnants of ridge and furrow, to a marker post. Already you can enjoy good views looking back over **Broadway**, with **Bredon Hill** in the distance. Pass through another metal gate and continue the climb, which is fairly gentle. Bear slightly right and head towards the top right corner of the field, to pass the National Trust sign for **Clump Farm**. Go over a modern wooden stile with a dog opening, by the old iron gate, and walk alongside a wonderful dry stone wall on the left. At a short steep stretch, make use of the steps and go over a stone slab stile with an iron bar. Pass a small group of magnificent old beech trees before another stile with a stone slab and metal bar. Walk on up the next field to a wooden stile and along a fenced track to pass to the left of the tower standing on top of the 1,027 ft (313 m) **Broadway Hill**. (1½ miles)

② Turn right through the tall deer-proof gate and enter **Broadway Country Park** to reach the 65 ft (20 m) tower, built as a folly in 1798 by the Earl of Coventry – to impress and please his wife! From the top of the tower are views over twelve counties.

Walk along the middle of the field looking for the red deer which live around here, and pass the memorial to commemorate the crash of an RAF bomber on a training mission on 2nd June 1943. Reach another tall gate and go onto the driveway and turn right. Pass to the right of the restaurant building, cross an area of grass, to a stile and onto the driveway. Turn right and walk past the **Rookery**, then fork right as the drive divides. It soon splits again and we keep straight ahead along a grassy track, which takes us downhill to a stony drive and into a small woodland area. At a T-junction, turn right to walk along a fairly level stretch, with good views down to the valley on the left and over towards Broadway. Just after passing the **Ledges**, bear slightly left and downhill across the field and into the woods. Before reaching a large gate, turn left along the track, (**Coneygree Lane**), into a narrow stretch of woodland with an abundance of wild flowers and bird life. Descending gradually, we reach the lodge house which is surrounded by a drift of snowdrops in February. (1¾ miles)

③ Turn right along **Snowshill Road**, and immediately on our left is the very old **St Eadburgha's** church.

The original church for Broadway, it dates from the 12th century and is situated on the old route from Worcester to London. Mounting steps are positioned just outside the churchyard gate and wildflowers, yew hedges and bushes add colour to the surroundings. This ancient church is well worth a visit before walking along the road, to pass another fine building on the left – Broadway Court. The gatehouse is all that remains of the former Court, where King Charles I stayed on two occasions.

On the right just past these buildings is the drive to **Lybrook Farm** and the footpath sign points us to the right. Walk away from the road for about 40 yards as far as the hedge, then turn left. Stay close to this hedge until it turns sharp right, then head across the open field to reach a wooden kissing gate. Continue straight ahead over the next field to another kissing gate, with good views to the Broadway church of **St Michael**. Keep straight ahead to reach a picnic and

THE 17TH-CENTURY PUB IN BROADWAY.

playground area. The path leads between fruit trees to a narrow path and a small public garden and out on to the main street in **Broadway**. Turn left along the main street, passing the major shops, and turn left along **Church Street**, to reach the **Crown and Trumpet**. (1½ miles)

④ After refreshment, continue along the road for half a mile (passing St Michael's church) and just beyond the houses of **Bury End** turn right along the narrow road. Before it bends to the right, go left, through a wooden kissing gate and follow the sign to **Brockhampton** and **Snowshill**. Cross the field to a wooden kissing gate by a large metal gate, and continue in the same direction as we climb up the next field. Ascending this large field we cross diagonally over an ancient ridge and furrow landscape, relic of farming in medieval times. In the top left corner of the field we reach a stile, with good views down to **St Eadburgha**.

Continue ahead, diagonally across the next field, and over another stile and up quite steeply, passing marker posts and aiming to the right of the edge of **Buckland Wood**. At the top, as the field levels off, reach a stile and follow the path as it heads across the middle of a large stony field, often used for crop growing – unlike most of the fields previously seen.

This is still a pastoral area, specialising in sheep. In former centuries, the sheep and especially the wool was the source of the wealth which financed the construction of many large houses, and also the many fine churches to be seen in the Cotswolds.

Cross the fairly flat field to a stile, and on across another large field, to reach two stiles and a stony track, the route of the **Cotswold Way**. Turn left here for a few yards and almost immediately turn right, following the sign to **Shenbarrow**, **Stanton** and the **Cotswold Way**. To our left are a house and farm buildings. Climbing slightly, we pass through a metal gate and follow the track which soon becomes grassy. Leave the track by going over a stile to the right, into a small wood. The narrow path descends, and leads on across pasture, over stiles and past a covered reservoir. The clear path leads us down towards the church, and to a small wooden kissing gate beyond which is the village road – and the church. (2¼ miles)

St Michael's church dates from the 13th century or earlier, and amongst its features of interest are the 15th-century tiles in the south aisle, the 16th-century maple wood mazer bowl and several stained-glass windows. The pews in the south aisle were known as shepherds' pews as local

shepherds came in via the west door and tied their dogs to the ends of the pews. Behind the church is Buckland Manor House, a 16th-century house, partially rebuilt in 1883, and now a hotel set in delightful gardens. The entire village is full of attractive houses and gardens.

⑤ From the church, turn right along the road, and just before it deteriorates to a track (the route of our arrival in **Buckland**), it rises slightly and we bend left, passing **Buckland Court** to our right. Follow the surfaced narrow road as it climbs. Small ponds are to the right, where moorhens, ducks and grey wagtails may be seen, and we pass the notice for **Burhill Farm**. Emerge above the trees, and as the track levels off, turn left to walk along the **Cotswold Way**.

Climb over two interesting stiles in a triangular framework by a metal gate, and after about 30 yards pass through a wooden gate, and turn left along the field margin. Soon reach a smart gate, and then another gate, but just keep ahead, following the field margin on our right, a very prolific hedge with crab apples, sloes and a wealth of food for birds. At the end of the field go through the modern metal kissing gate and bend right into the woods, **Broadway Coppice**. Descend through this old woodland along a stone floored path, and at a gate leave the wood to walk along the left margin of an open field, with good views right to Broadway with its prominent church tower. Follow the left margin as the path bends right, to lead us down to a metal kissing gate and a narrow path. Reach a gate and cross the road to another gate, and keep ahead across the fields heading towards the church tower – and soon reach the road, with Point 4, the pub and **St Michael's** church a few yards to the left. Cross straight over and follow the path through a wooden kissing gate. The town centre car park can be seen to the left, and turn here to pass through a modern shopping development to reach **High Street**. Turn right and walk along as far as **Leamington Road**, then turn left to return to our starting point. (2¼ miles)

Date walk completed:

MIDDLE LITTLETON TO CLEEVE PRIOR

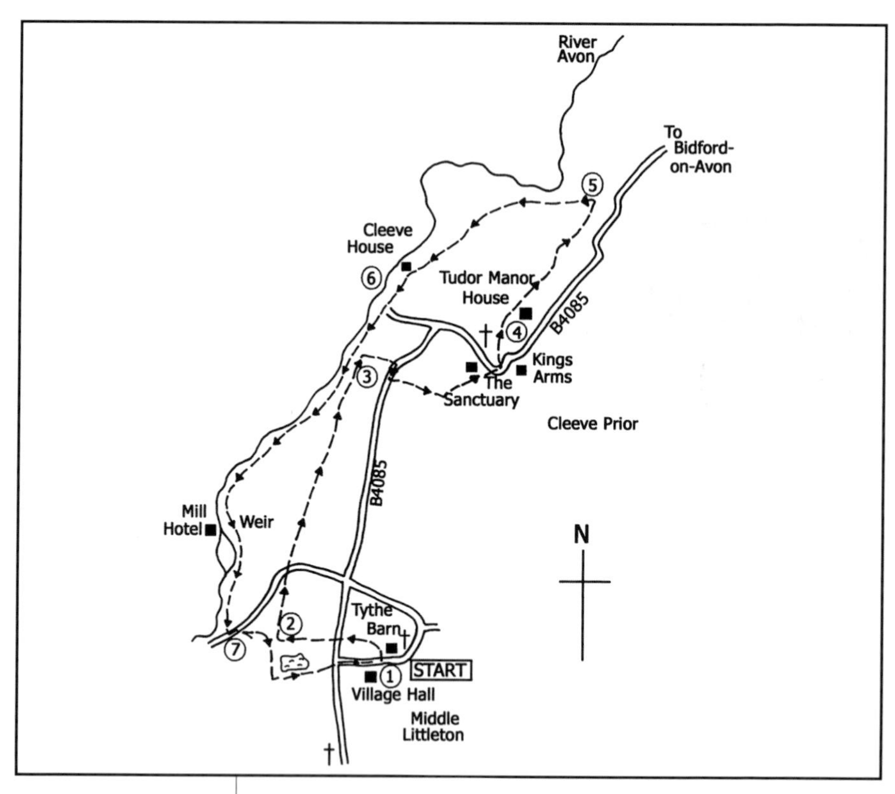

Distance:
$9\frac{3}{4}$ miles

Starting point:
The village hall in Middle Littleton. GR 078469

Maps: OS Landranger 150 Worcester, the Malverns and surrounding area; or OS Explorer 205 Stratford-upon-Avon and Evesham

How to get there: *Middle Littleton is reached from Evesham along the B4035 towards Badsey and Bretforton. At Badsey, turn left on the B4085 to the Littletons. Pass through South Littleton and at Middle Littleton turn right towards the church and tithe barn. Just before reaching these buildings, there is a parking area on the right by the village hall.*

THE MEDIEVAL TITHE BARN IN MIDDLE LITTLETON.

The village of Middle Littleton is sandwiched between North and South Littleton in the intensively farmed Vale of Evesham. Fruit and vegetables grow in the fields and the River Avon is always close by, providing delightful scenery as we walk round this group of east Worcestershire villages, close to the Warwickshire border. The outlier of Cotswold limestone which created Cleeve Hill adds variety to the scenery and natural history. The Worcestershire Wildlife Trust manages both the Cleeve Prior and Windmill Hill Nature Reserves which we see on this circuit. Windmill Hill is mainly grassland and home to many flowers, butterflies and birds, whereas much of the Cleeve Prior reserve has reverted to woodland and attracts different wildlife. The name Cleeve is derived from the Anglo Saxon word for a cliff, a prominent feature of this walk.

The Kings Arms in Cleeve Prior dates from 1547, or earlier, perhaps from the 12th century, and a local rumour mentions the existence of a ghost in residence. From the delightful garden at the rear can be seen the ancient dove holes in the barn.

Food is served daily *except on Mondays and the choice ranges from home-cooked main meals to well filled sandwiches. Sunday lunch is particularly popular, and booking is advisable. It is also the pub for the locals, and the most popular beer is the real ale from Hobsons. Telephone: 01789 773335*

① From the lay-by close to the village hall in **Middle Littleton**, walk along the road towards the church, but before reaching the church turn left along a stony track following the footpath sign to **Cleeve Prior** and the **tithe barn**.

The medieval tithe barn dates from the 13th century and was the property of the Abbots of Evesham. It was given to the National Trust in 1975, and subsequently restored and is still in use – but is open daily to visitors in the afternoons from April to the end of October. Telephone 01905 371006.

At the end of the lane go over a stile by a large gate then turn left along the field margin, with houses and gardens to our left. After two fields reach the road which we cross and keep straight ahead over a stile and along the right margin of the field. Continue ahead through a metal gate, with market gardening to our right and following a line of fruit trees. Climbing very slightly we reach a bridleway where we turn right. Take care here as it can be muddy or churned up by horses! (1 mile)

② It is a level stretch, with a hedge and fields to the right, and the escarpment slopes steeply down to our left. Excellent views to the left over the **River Avon** take in **Wood Norton** with a mast on the hilltop – and the **Malverns** in the distance beyond. Diagonally ahead and down on the plain is the green spire of **Harvington** church. As we pass an information board on the left, we reach the end of the **Windmill Hill Nature Reserve**.

For more than 400 years the limestone hillside has been covered with grass and scrub and is particularly rich in wildflowers, butterflies and many large anthills built up by the yellow meadow ants.

Walking on, we reach a road and turn right for 20 yards, then left again passing a house called **The Hills**, to continue along the bridleway still heading north. There is now a wood on the slope to our left. After about a mile we reach an open patch where a path goes back and down to our left – but keep ahead along the level bridleway for a further 200 yards. Then turn right where a large post has the name of the **Greenlink**. (1½ miles)

③ Walk along a field margin – with the hedge on our left. At the end of this field, turn right along the road for about 100 yards and then turn left at a finger post with the snail logo. Cross the middle of a large open field, and at the far side of this field go through the large wooden gate with the name **Quarry Furlong**. We are entering the **Millennium Woodland**. Head diagonally across the field, in the direction of the church tower clearly seen ahead. At the far side of this field is the notice-board for **Cleeve Prior Millennium Green** and we leave through the gate, cross the drive and go straight ahead through a small gate. Pass the **Sanctuary**, with its pond, hides and seats, on our left, and climb over the stile and keep ahead across the next field, with the church now away to our left. Cross over the next stile, and one more field, to reach the road. Turn right to the **Kings Arms**. (1¼ miles)

④ From the pub turn right and walk along the road for about 100 yards. As the road bends right beyond the last houses of the village, turn left before **Manor Court**, along the

THE KINGS ARMS IN CLEEVE PRIOR.

narrow path between walls. Just before the church, turn right for the onward route, and head for a gap through the line of poplars.

But before doing so, go on past the church to enjoy the sight of the old and delightful houses which surround the small green. Also, the church is well worth a visit. Dating from Norman times it has seen many subsequent changes, including the Gothic windows of 1863. The font is 14th-century and the nave roof timbers are medieval.

From the church go through the line of poplars and cross the overflow churchyard to a metal kissing gate. The magnificent **Tudor manor house** is to our right, and like the church, the pub and several other old buildings, has been built of the local liassic limestone – evidence of the proximity of the Cotswolds. Keep straight ahead along the clear path to a footbridge and stile and then along the left margin of the next field. Reach a metal kissing gate and keep straight ahead to continue along the left side of a very stony field (Cotswold stone fragments). Pass through another metal kissing gate, and along the right side of the next field. The path bends left, and then goes right, through a gap in the hedge. Follow a broad grassy path and when it bends right, keep ahead along the path to a stile in the hedge and then slightly left to a stile at the left corner of the next field. Cross a small field and begin to go downhill slightly (towards the small village of **Marlcliff**, with views to **Bidford-on-Avon** and its prominent church tower nearly one mile away) to another stile and then a steep descent down some steps. (1¼ miles)

⑤ At the foot of the steps and before reaching buildings and a track, turn left on a grassy track (which may be muddy as it is a bridleway) and climb steeply. Reach a fairly level and narrow field, and at the end go through an old gate and along the bridleway between hedges. Walk on to another old iron gate and then emerge into an open field, with woods and a steep slope going down to the right. When we reach a hedge straight ahead, take the right side along the top of an open field sloping down to the river. Stay close to the hedge on the left, and then on to another stretch of narrow path, between fence and hedge. This leads us through to a track and an old wind pump on our right. Keep straight ahead along the narrow path between hedges, to reach a wooden gate and a house (**Cleeve House**) on the right. Beyond the gate is a surfaced driveway and when we reach another house on the right, we can take the steps down to the river or alternatively keep straight ahead until reaching a narrow road, and then turn right to walk down to the river. At the riverbank turn left. A large caravan site can be seen on the opposite bank and a bridge links this site to an island in mid river. (1½ miles)

⑥ From the small car parking area by the river, walk downstream with a steep wooded slope on our left. Numerous platforms on the other bank are for the use of fishermen – a very popular spot. Ducks, Canada geese and swans are common along here, and there may be a few cormorants, plus a fleeting glimpse of a kingfisher. Pass a stile and keep ahead, and reach a small iron gate where a path comes down from the left. The river now bends away to the right and so the wooded slope retreats away to the left as we enter open fields. A large rookery may be seen and heard up on the steep slope. Pass a fishing pond on the left as we follow the riverbank, through two large fields and then several smaller fields, over stiles or through gaps in the field boundaries. We reach the end of the Birmingham Angling area and move on to the Offenham Park Angling Club territory. Just before the weir, notice the **Mill Hotel** across the river, and then use two stiles and a footbridge to pass a wooden house on our right. Walk on along the stony drive, as it leads towards the large caravan site seen from the hilltop earlier in the walk. Pass between the very smart caravans, mostly raised off the ground to reduce danger from flooding. As we leave the caravan park we reach a narrow road. (2 miles)

⑦ The **Fish and Anchor** pub is about 300 yards away to the right, but we turn left for 20 yards and then right over a stile and diagonally left across the field. Reach a stile where we enter the **Windmill Hill Nature Reserve** and climb steeply up to the bridleway where we walked earlier. Turn right along this bridleway and follow the level path to reach a junction of tracks. We turn left here along a broad track, with a small reservoir about 50 yards away to our left. Pass the large buildings of Kanes Food on our right, and when we reach the road go straight across along **School Lane** to walk back to the car. (1¼ miles)

Date walk completed:

Walk 5

PERSHORE TO TIDDESLEY AND WICK

PERSHORE'S 14TH-CENTURY BRIDGE.

Distance:
10 miles

Starting point:
Pershore old bridge GR 953451 (alternative could be GR 929462 – at entrance to Tiddesley wood)

**Maps: OS Explorer 190 Malvern Hills and Bredon Hill;
OS Landranger 150 Worcester, the Malverns and surrounding area**

How to get there: *Pershore is easily reached from Worcester, Evesham or Upton upon Severn. The starting point at the old bridge is about 500 yards from the town centre, along the main road leading towards Evesham – the B4084 (formerly A44).*

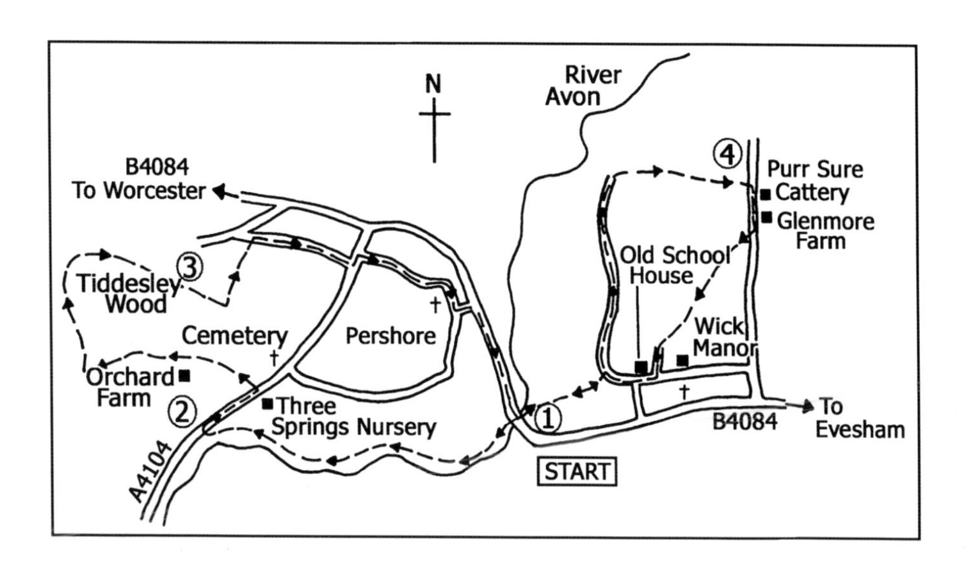

The delightful small market town of Pershore is sited alongside the River Avon, and we start and finish the walk in the town, as well as walking along the riverbank. The main street is lined with 17th and 18th-century Georgian buildings, but dominating the town is the abbey, built of local limestone and founded in AD 689 by King Oswald. King Edgar granted it to the Benedictines in AD 972, though nothing remains from the monastery and only the choir remains from the original church. The magnificent chancel contains arcades dating from 1230, built after the fire of 1223. Mostly flat or gently undulating, the walk leads along riverbanks through woods and across meadows and cropped fields. Wildflowers in the woods and field margins and cultivated flowers grown by one farmer, as well as the almost ever-present view to the 14th-century tower of the wonderful Pershore abbey, help to enhance this rural landscape.

The Brandy Cask is a freehouse and a regular in each year's Camra Good Beer Guide. The beer is brewed on the premises and includes Whistling Joe (3.6%), Brandy Snapper (4%) and John Baker Original (4.8%). Situated on the main street in a Georgian building dating from 1779, this is a very popular pub with the locals, as well as visitors.

Food is served daily *except on Tuesdays, and the choice is full meals, jacket potatoes or bar snacks, which may be eaten in the bar or small restaurant or in the landscaped gardens which stretch down to the river, where there is also a mooring for boats. Telephone 01386 552602.*

Pershore's old 14th-century bridge bears evidence of the Civil War but also has an information board about a more recent war – World War II. About half a mile out of town beyond the bridge is the Pershore College of Horticulture – well worth a visit for any keen gardeners.

① From the car park and picnic place walk back to the main road, cross over with care and turn right along the main road. Once over the river, go left following the sign for the **Pershore Bridges Circular Walk** along the riverbank.

The River Avon rises near Naseby, the site of another battle, and flows for 112 miles to join the Severn at Tewkesbury. A popular boating river, it is navigable from Alveston (near Stratford) to Tewkesbury.

Soon reach a small gate, alongside the large iron gate, but keep ahead. Boats will be anchored across the river and a few houses sit on the slope opposite – enjoying views over to **Pershore abbey**. A young mixed deciduous wood is on our right, with hazel, ash, oak, beech and alder. At the end of the field and wood, cross the ditch over a footbridge but continue along the riverbank. Over to the right is a good view to the abbey, which we will continue to see from different angles throughout this walk. Keep ahead through several fields, which are separated by drainage ditches – in this wet and occasionally flooded landscape. Some of the fields are kept as grass but others are cropped on the fertile silty soil. **Bredon Hill** is over to our left, ahead is **Tiddesley Wood** on the hill, and the spire of **Pershore** cemetery chapel is over to the right. As the river and our path become closer to the main road, the river wanders on to **Tewkesbury**, but we turn right, following the sign for the **Avon Valley Circular Walk**. Walk alongside the ditch up to the iron gate, and the road A4104.
(1¾ miles)

② Turn right to walk along the verge for 300 yards and opposite the **Three Springs Nursery** go left along the public bridleway, signed to **Tiddesley Wood**. This leads up to the delightful thatched black and white **Woodman's Cottage**. Our path passes through the small gate to the right of the house, and heads to the stile by two metal gates in the right corner of the field. Continue towards the woods with a hedge and ditch to our left. The buildings of **Orchard Farm** are away to our left. Enter the woods over the stile by a gate and an information board, and immediately there is a choice of three paths. Take the middle route, a bridleway track, straight ahead in a westerly direction. Once on this track it bends slightly right and then begins to descend. Drop down to a very clear cross track (the main route through the middle of the wood in a north-south direction). Cross straight over this track. Several recently cleared areas along here are part of the ongoing management of the woods, always aiming to keep a variety of habitat for different wildlife. Reach a few fir trees and keep straight ahead at a crosspath. Before beginning to descend towards the edge of the woods, notice a flagpole on the left of the path, with a warning notice about firing. A few yards beyond here we turn right, over a stile, to walk along the top edge of a field, with the woods on our right – and the small **Bow Brook** down to our left. Follow the edge of the woods, passing two orchards on our left. As the wood ends, a path goes left down towards the river and an orchard is straight ahead but we turn right, just inside the edge of the wood. Walk along this narrow path, and reach the main broad path near the entrance to the woods – and the car park (GR 929462) is up to the left along the track. (2 miles)

Tiddesley (or Tyddesley) Wood is very old woodland, growing on

THE BRANDY CASK IN PERSHORE.

clay soils (hence the muddy areas) with patches of river gravel on top. The wood has existed since the Ice Age, and was mentioned in the Domesday Book. At that time it was common land, used for pig grazing, though later became enclosed as a deer park. The Forestry Commission took over in 1952 and some conifers were planted, but in 1984 most of the wood was taken over by the Worcestershire Wildlife Trust. A firing range remains in the south-west corner. The wood is managed for the variety of wildlife, notably flowers (especially bluebells), butterflies (including white admirals and peacocks) and birds. The wide range of trees includes the original Pershore egg plum. The wood is different with each season, but there is always something interesting to see or hear. On my last visit, in midwinter, I heard a tawny owl calling, in the middle of the day – presumably being disturbed and mobbed by small birds.

③ Keep straight ahead across the main track, through the metal gate to walk along the right side of a field, with the woods on the right. Keep ahead through two more fields to reach the top of the slope. Pass the end of the wood and good views open up to the top of the abbey tower and to **Bredon Hill**. Continue along the field boundary as far as a T-junction where we turn left and follow the fence on our right, across open land. Head towards the buildings in the distance, and emerge on to a road. Turn right here, with houses on our left and an open field on our right. Follow this road, as it begins to descend, and at the major road, turn left for about 30 yards, and then turn right to walk along **Newlands**, signed 'to the Abbey'. Pass to the left of the abbey. Turn left along **Broad Street** which is really a small market square, and, at the end of this, turn right along **Bridge Street** passing through the centre of **Pershore**. About half a mile along here we reach the old bridge and our starting point – but on this road we pass the **Brandy Cask**. Look out for the penultimate building at the edge of Pershore – the **old toll house** – with a copy of charges still visible. (2½ miles)

(Back to point 1 again) This is really the halfway point of the walk and, after a look at the information board, (information about World War II defences as well as older times), continue by taking the footpath signed to **Wick**. Go through the kissing gate, and follow the narrow surfaced path across the middle of the field, often full of grazing sheep. After another kissing gate and cattle grid, continue straight ahead along the footpath between hedges. At the narrow road turn left, passing a few houses on the right, and walk along this country lane for nearly three quarters of a mile, between fields of cereals, rape and perhaps sunflowers. At the end of this road, just past the old barns on the left and the house on the right, fork right following the footpath sign, and head across a grassy paddock to a stile in the far left corner of the field. Once over this stile move a few yards left and keep ahead alongside the hedge. At the end of this field move 20 yards to the left and then turn right alongside the hedge. This will lead to a stiled footbridge. Keep ahead along the right margin of the next field, passing a few fine willow trees. Continue over a stile and footbridge, and keep ahead, towards the buildings across this field. Pass between the house and the barns of **Owletts Farm**, to reach a narrow road, where we turn right. (2 miles)

④ Along this road we soon pass the **Purr Sure cattery**, with its large wooden cat in the garden, and then reach **Glenmore Farm** on the left, where we turn right. The footpath is straight for 100 yards before bending to the left, and we follow this track between cropped fields. The second field on the right grew larkspur in 2004, for use as confetti. **Pershore abbey** in the background makes this a very photogenic spot. The track leads on to a narrow road and into the village of **Wick**. At the bigger road, by the **Old School House,** turn right.

An interesting short detour to the left could take you to the small Norman church of St Mary's – much restored in 1861 and 1893. Opposite the church is the magnificent Wick Manor looking old, though only built in 1923. Also, there are a few genuinely old, timber-framed houses in the village.

Having turned right, we walk along the road. Pass two left turns, **Yock Lane** bends to the right, and we soon reach our path on the left, where we turn to retrace steps along the paved footpath back to the start. (1 3/4 miles)

Date walk completed:

CROOME, PIRTON AND KINNERSLEY

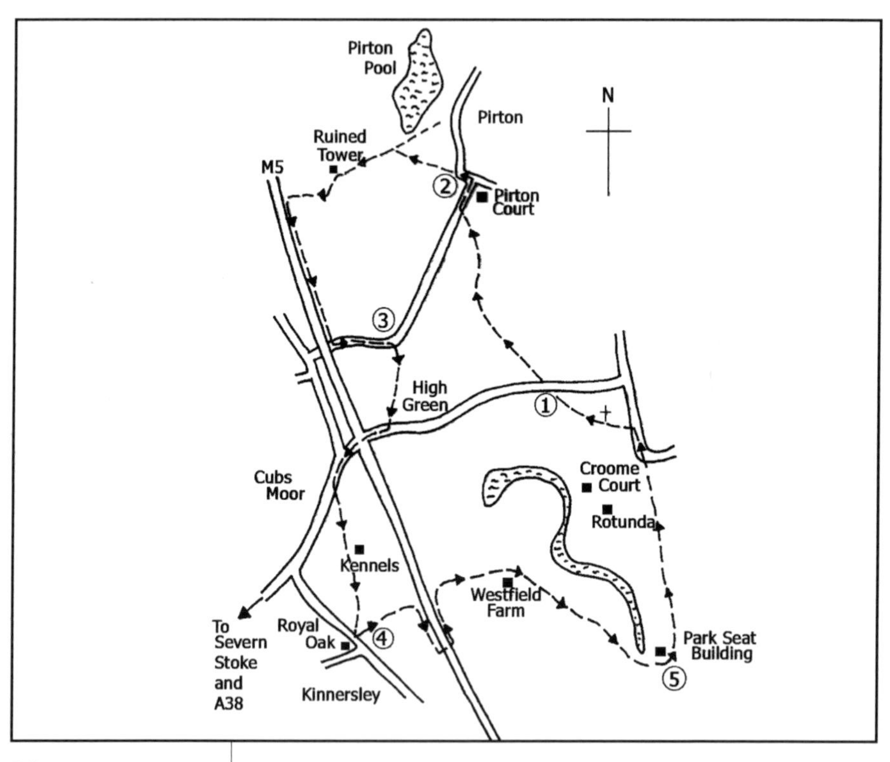

Distance:
9 miles

Starting point:
Lay-by in Croome. GR 883453

Maps: OS Explorer 190 Malvern Hills and Bredon Hill; or Landranger 150 Worcester, the Malverns and surrounding area

How to get there: *From the A38 Worcester to Tewkesbury road, turn off just south of Severn Stoke following a sign to Kinnersley and Croome. In Kinnersley, by the Royal Oak, turn left at the T-junction, signed to Croome. After nearly a mile along here, turn right, cross over the motorway and, once beyond High Green, the site of the Croome Estate Office, look for the lay-by on the right side of the road.*

THE CHURCH OF ST MARY MAGDALENE IN CROOME.

This is a walk across farmland and parkland that takes us through Croome Park, with its superb collection of trees, buildings and viewpoints. It was the 6th Earl of Coventry who pursued the programme of landscape improvement in the mid 18th century. Over 500 varieties of tree were planted originally, and Croome was second only to Kew for its collection of trees. After years of neglect, the National Trust acquired most of the park in 1996 and is now nearing the end of a ten-year restoration project, which aims to return the landscape to its 19th-century appearance. Much of the restoration can be seen on the walk, but more of the park can be visited from the National Trust visitors' car park. Croome Court is set in the midst of the landscape created by Capability Brown, who aimed to convert the existing agricultural scenery into a vision of 'Ideal Nature'. This was his first complete landscape and made his reputation. It was copied in many other locations throughout Britain.

The Royal Oak is the village pub of Kinnersley which has had links with horse racing for many years. Stables are still found in the village and the pub contains exciting memorabilia of famous names in racing, including the Rimells and Venetia Williams.

This delightful village pub *is open seven days a week serving excellent food, real ales such as Wye Valley and Bombardier, and fine wines.*
The Acorns restaurant offers an à la carte menu and there is a lunchtime menu (from 12 noon to 2 pm) and bar snacks to satisfy hungry walkers.
Telephone: 01905 371482.

The Walk

① From the lay-by, cross the road and walk diagonally left across the field passing to the right of a small wood, where bluebells grow in spring and pheasants are reared. Go over a stile and along the left margin of the next field, with the small pond on our right. At the end of the field, pass the National Trust Croome Park sign, and move slightly left and immediately right alongside the hedge and wood. Walk on through a gap in the hedge, into a small shrubby area to reach a plank footbridge. Cross the next two fields, aiming to the left of the large house ahead (**Pirton Court**). At the road turn right, to pass Pirton Court.
(1 mile)

The 16th-century, half-timbered Pirton Court was built on the site of a medieval moated manor. It was owned from 1592 by the Coventry family, one of whom invited visiting Test cricketers here in the 1930s, whilst they were playing their matches against Worcestershire.

② The road bends left, where it is joined by the narrow road from **Croome**, and after 20 yards it bends right but we go left here along the footpath. Cross the field to a small gate and continue up the slope towards the Gothic tower (specially built as a ruin). On the left is a curving fence, the end of the former racecourse, and as we climb the hill we are joined by the path coming from **Pirton Pool** down to our right. At present there is no stile across the fence on our left and so continue to the top of the field and turn left through the gate to walk along the line of fine cedars and pass the ruined tower. Go through the gate and on reaching the end of the narrow wood, turn right to descend alongside the fence (admiring the views of the **Malverns** in the distance) to a small gate, and keep ahead with the hedge on our left. Just before the motorway turn left through the gate, and walk alongside with the motorway on the right for three fields. Veer slightly left to two gates near a mast, and walk on to the road. Turn left here and proceed for 300 yards to where the road is bending left. (2 miles)

③ At this point, turn right along a bridleway and then onto the track passing farm buildings in **High Green**, to reach another road. Turn right and cross over the motorway. There is a footpath going left alongside the motorway but we go on to the T-junction and then turn left. Over to our right are good views to the **Panorama Tower** (by Adam 1766) on top of **Cubs Moor**. Once past the small lodge house on the left, go left along the footpath signed across the field, to pass to the right of the walled area around some kennels and continue to a stile in the far right corner of the field. Our onward path goes left across the same field, but, if in need of sustenance, cross the stile and turn left to reach the **Royal Oak**. (1 3/4 miles)

④ From the pub, retrace your steps to the stile 80 yards along the road, and notice there are two footpaths. Take the right-hand path, crossing the field towards the M5. Pass through a small scrubby area to the right of a pond. Emerging into another field, the path leads diagonally left and at the far end of this field turn right alongside the M5. At the end of this field, cross the motorway and proceed along the field margin, with the motorway now on the left. Go through a gap in the hedge, and head diagonally right across the field towards the trees, one of several small woodlands on the Croome Estate. Pass the **Croome Park** sign and, beyond the narrow belt of trees, turn right along the field margin. At the end of the field go through the kissing gate, and straight across a small field to the farm drive, with the buildings of **Westfield Farm** to the right. Cross the farm road to a kissing gate and, although the original footpath leads diagonally right across the middle of a very

THE VILLAGE PUB IN KINNERSLEY

large field, it is recommended to keep straight on through a metal gate.

Ahead are wonderful views to Croome Court, St Mary Magdalene church and, to the left of the church, the small woodland in which are located several parkland buildings, including the Temple Greenhouse with its pillars, built by Robert Adam in 1760.

Walk to the narrow lake, named **Croome River**, and turn right. Walk alongside this haven for wildlife, to the far corner of the field, and notice the **Park Seat** building visible through a gap in the trees on the slope ahead. Leave the field via a stile, and pass over a stream and alongside a small pond. ($2^1/_2$ miles)

In this wetland area a variety of plants and bushes grow, including a few plane trees which, even in winter, still contain their fruits, as these do not break open until the spring, when they release their seeds.

⑤ Reach a gate and then a stile at the margin of **Croome Park**. Climb the short steep slope alongside the bushes to the left, but look over to the right beyond the large barn where **Dunstall Castle** (another specially-built ruin) can be seen. Once over the stile at the top, follow the field margin on our left. After about 100 yards, turn left through an old gateway and re-enter Croome Park to follow the path straight ahead. But first make a detour to the left, to visit the Park Seat building, with its magnificent views across the lake.

Our path leads through a few trees to a stile beyond which we follow the field margin to the right, along the edge of the wood. Then keep straight ahead through open fields, with good views to Croome Court.

Most of the interior of Croome Court was designed by Robert Adam and James Wyatt, though Capability Brown may have had a small hand in it. Started in 1751, it was built of Bath stone to a Palladian design.

To the right are all the QinetiQ (formerly DERA) screens and spheres at the Government Research station at **Defford**. As we come alongside a line of old oak trees, just keep straight ahead to the end of the field and a patch of trees and bushes. The **Rotunda** (built 1753-56) is in these trees to our left. We reach the road, near the **London Arch**, the main entrance (private) to Croome Park and Court.

Go straight ahead along the road for about 200 yards, and turn left through a small kissing gate onto the footpath leading to the church. To the right of the church is the garden recently restored by the National Trust. An information board shows some of the features to be seen in the magnificent view across the park towards the **Malvern Hills** and **Pirton Tower**.

The old church of St Mary Magdalene was demolished by Capability Brown, when he was laying out the park, and he designed and built the present church, dedicated in 1763, in an imposing position on top of the hill. The interior of the church was designed by Robert Adam in 1761-62, and contains 17th-century Coventry memorials brought from the old church. The church is now owned and maintained by the Churches Conservation Trust.

From the information board, turn to the right and walk alongside the fence (and the gate into the shrubbery and the National Trust car park and reception area) for about 20 yards to reach a wooden kissing gate in the corner. Turn sharp left and walk downhill alongside the wooden fence. Across to our left can be seen a small wood and the evergreen shrubbery, and on the lower slopes and the flatter ground is an area of recent planting. Beyond this and across the ha-ha is the stump of the last Brownian oak and the new sapling oak tree planted by Chris Beardshaw in 2003, to replace the large dead oak tree, a survivor from Capability Brown's time.

As we descend the slope, admire the views across to the house before passing between the fence and a small pond on our right. Beyond here, go diagonally right, towards the far corner of the field and a stile by the large wooden gate to reach the starting point. As we head across this last field we can look into the woods to our left, where the old Pleasure Ground is being restored to its former condition and the buildings are also being restored. If you have an hour or so to wander round this area, why not drive to the National Trust car park and obtain a ticket for an extension to the walk. (1¾ miles)

Date walk completed:

Walk 7

NORTHERN MALVERN HILLS

THE NAG'S HEAD IN MALVERN.

Distance:
$8\frac{3}{4}$ miles

Starting point:
Church Street, Great Malvern, near the Tourist Information Centre. GR 775459

Maps: OS Explorer 190 Malvern Hills and Bredon Hill; or Sheet 1 of the set of 3 maps at a 1:10,000 scale published by the Map Shop in Upton and available at the shop or from the Tourist Information Centre

How to get there: *Great Malvern is reached from the M5 via Worcester and the A449 or from Upton upon Severn and the A4104. Signs direct you to the car parks (payment necessary) in Great Malvern either near the Splash swimming pool, or behind the Waitrose store. From either of these car parks, walk uphill along the main shopping street (Church Street) to reach the Tourist Information Centre.*

Malvern is famous for its hills, springs, the Priory church, and the home of the radar research establishment (now called QinetiQ) whose work was crucial in the Second World War. This walk takes us to the hills and past eight springs, whilst providing views of the church and QinetiQ. We complete a circuit of the hills, through woods and onto the open hilltop, enjoying wonderful views over Worcestershire, Herefordshire and, on a clear day, long distance views in all directions from the top of the Worcestershire Beacon. Some steep, though short, stretches are encountered as we climb or descend the hills.

The Nags Head is a lively and popular pub, with a recently enlarged and refurbished restaurant area. The pub is close to the end of the walk, but there are seats and suitable picnic stops at regular intervals on the route.

Excellent food for lunches *or evening meals is on offer at the pub, with the cooked selection including steak pie with Hereford beef and fresh vegetables, or local sausages in a variety of flavours. As for the beers, the choice is endless. Telephone: 01684 574373.*

The Walk

① From **Great Malvern** station or the main car parks, walk to the top of **Church Street**, near the post office and Tourist Information Centre. Cross over to **Belle Vue Gardens**, with the Elgar statue and the Malvhina spring. Use the pedestrian crossing to walk on past Lloyds (with its Civic Society plaque) and the Mount Pleasant (also involved in the Water Cure in Victorian times). Climb the 99 steps and on up the road which winds steeply up to **St Ann's Well**.

There are refreshments if required and information plaques about the blind pianist who played here, as well as the history of the spring.

Continue the ascent round the back of the buildings and follow the track to where it divides. Turn sharp left and, after a few yards, left again, along the track passing above **St Ann's Well**. This broad track climbs steadily out of the woods and on through the open hillside. When we reach a sharp elbow bend, where there is a bench to the left, keep straight ahead along a narrow path. This leads over a few rocky outcrops as it undulates round

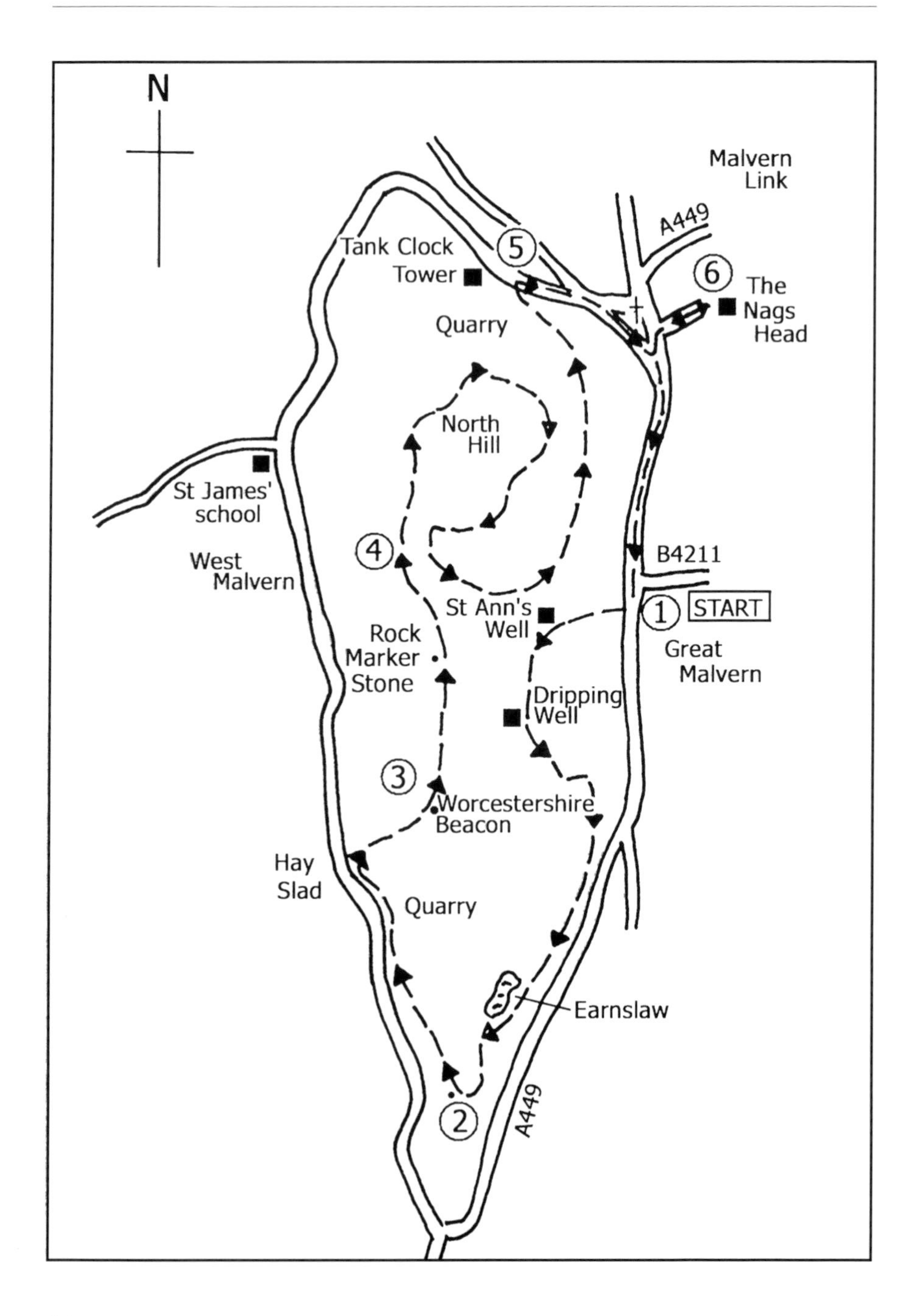
N
Malvern
Link
A449
Tank Clock
Tower
5
6
The
Nags
Head
Quarry
North
Hill
St James'
school
4
West
Malvern
B4211
St Ann's
Well
1
START
Great
Malvern
Rock
Marker
Stone
Dripping
Well
3
Worcestershire
Beacon
Hay
Slad
Quarry
Earnslaw
2
A449

to the far side of **Rushy Valley**, one of the steepest and most impressive valleys on the **Malvern Hills**. This river-formed valley was probably enlarged by ice during the Ice Age. As the path bends left round the far side of the valley, look out for the **Dripping Well** on the right of the path, one of the highest springs (at 1,020 ft/310 m) on the hills, and which keeps trickling even in prolonged spells of dry weather. This spring is very popular with birds for drinking or bathing and a linnet, stonechat or robin may be seen here. Views are good down into the valley and over part of the town, including the former Imperial Hotel, now part of the girls' college, built at the time of the arrival of the railway line. The path bends right round a rocky outcrop, to head southwards – and down to our left at the foot of the hills can be seen the main buildings of **Malvern College**, with its extensive playing fields stretching out across the plain. Follow the path as it contours along the hillside, descending slightly, and just past a backless iron seat, the path bends quite sharply round to the left and leads on down to a nearly horizontal major track. Here we turn right and follow this broad and gravelled path in a southerly direction. Pass the memorial seat to Con and Lena, then veer away from the road, following the sign to **Wyche Cutting**. Ascend steadily through the woods to emerge at an open patch near the **Earnslaw** quarry lake. To visit the lake, go slightly right and pass an information board, but our onward route is to the far left of this open patch.

Here a few steps lead to the viewpoint over the lake and in the rocky debris across the foot of the steep slope is the spring which is its source of water.

Follow the path at the bottom of the steps, not the broad level track but the ascending path into the woods. After 20 yards this splits and we take the right fork and climb steadily. The path leads us to a stone marker at the **Gold Mine**, where we reach the main path from **Wyche Cutting** to the **Worcestershire Beacon**. ($2^1/_4$ miles)

This is surfaced now, as a result of wear and tear and erosion in the past, but is also useful for any emergency vehicles.

② Go straight across this surfaced track to the path which immediately turns right passing the memorial seat to a Mr Herbert Skeys. We are entering a different world with different views. This is the west side of the ridge and vistas over Herefordshire and into Wales open up – a more undulating and often greener sight than looking over

Worcestershire and the Severn Plain. Descend steadily back into woods, on a broad path, and when the path divides, fork right and climb for a short distance. Then reach a level grassy patch, with the back wall of a large quarry to the right. This is one of the group of quarries called the West of England quarries, purchased by the Conservators in 1931, and gradually landscaped since that time. Descend from the grassy path to a stony track which leads into the large quarry – but we keep ahead along the fairly horizontal path and soon reach the first car parking area. At the far side of this, three tracks go ahead. (The left path is the surfaced car parking route, the middle is for 'Residents Only' and the third and right path goes up past the 'Authorised Vehicles Only' sign.) Before taking this right hand of the three routes – turn sharp left across the surfaced track to the footpath leading down through the trees to the road – and more importantly, to **Hay Slad**, one of the most powerful springs on the hills.

THE TANK CLOCK TOWER, NEAR THE NORTH MALVERN QUARRIES.

A popular spot for locals and visitors, Hay Slad holds a never-ending supply of water

and has a never-ending supply of visitors arriving with their empty bottles.

After visiting **Hay Slad**, we retrace our steps to the broad grassy track with the 'Authorised Vehicles Only' sign. Climb steadily through trees, with old quarries on our right, and at a sharp elbow, bend right to follow the track. We gradually move out above the trees. The slope to our left is mainly covered by gorse and bracken. Note the long view ahead to the stepped profile of the Herefordshire Beacon (**British Camp**), with the obelisk to the right of this hill. The path levels off to reach a seat on our left, where the main path keeps ahead, but we turn sharp left on a narrower path. We are now climbing up a steep slope but the zigzag of the path makes the slope less testing, and we can soon see the buildings of **West Malvern**, with the large house at **St James's School** being most prominent. We gradually climb up towards the **Worcestershire Beacon** and when we reach a broad stony path, by a wooden bench, turn right and continue up to the summit of the Worcestershire Beacon (1,394 ft/425 m). (1 1/4 miles)

Enjoy the wide and stunning views, with locations marked and named on the toposcope, a memorial to Queen Victoria's Diamond Jubilee. There are vistas along the ridge to the south, and looking north is North Hill (1,305 ft/397 m) where we are going next, with the path leading to a col, between North Hill and Table Hill (1,225 ft/373 m).

③ Several paths lead down to the same point and we simply descend in a northerly direction, along any of the paths and as the steep descent eases gradually, we come alongside the ditch and ridge.

This is the Red Earl's Shire Ditch which dates from 1287-1291. The Red Earl was Gilbert de Clare, Earl of Gloucester and he created this boundary to prevent his deer crossing into the land owned by the Bishop of Hereford.

Descend to the round Malvern granite marker stone, with direction arrows. Keep straight ahead following the arrow to **North Hill**, along the broad gravel track on the right side of **Sugarloaf Hill**. The top of **Happy Valley** slopes down to our right and **Great Malvern** comes into sight. (1/2 mile)

④ Once past this valley, the track bends round to the right of **North Hill** (the route of our return) but we keep straight ahead up the grassy slope and over the col, then drop down the other side to a clear track running round **North Hill**. This is the Lady Howard de Walden Drive (created in the 1890s), and we turn right here to follow this broad track. It is a fairly horizontal route though it has to rise slightly as it bends round to the right, in order to pass above the top of the North Malvern quarries. The plain of Worcestershire comes into view here, as we say farewell to the views west to Herefordshire. Walk on round **North Hill** and the **de Walden Way** leads us back to the top of **Happy Valley** where we turn left to descend quite steeply towards **St Ann's Well** and **Great Malvern**. Pass another spring on the right of this path. As we descend, you will notice that part of this track is stony – this was once an important route across the hills to **West Malvern**. The avenue of sycamore was planted in the 1930s. At a junction of paths, a driveway goes right to St Ann's but we go left along the broad path to **Ivyscar** rocks. Continue on beyond this large outcrop, and gradually slope down to the North Malvern quarries. The first, with the car park, is **Scar Quarry**, but walk along the road past the **Tank Clock Tower** to visit the **Tank quarry**, with its high back wall and a small geological exhibition on the flat floor of the quarry. (3 miles)

⑤ We retrace our steps to the road and walk back towards **Malvern** town centre. Pass **Holy Trinity** church on the left, and on the opposite side of the road are some stocks, an animal pound and an old spring. At the main road, turn sharp left, cross over and walk along the pavement. Pass the top of **Bank Street** and just before reaching the **Morgan**, an interesting pub with a collection of memorabilia of the Morgan car factory, turn right down **Lygon Bank**. This will lead to the **Nags Head** pub. (1 mile)

⑥ After refreshment, walk along the other side of the pub, up **Bank Street** to return to the main road. Turn left here and, passing the old Victorian houses which line the main road, arrive back in the centre of **Great Malvern**. (3/4 mile)

Date walk completed:

KNIGHTWICK

KNIGHTWICK CHAPEL, NOW USED AS A CEMETERY CHAPEL.

Distance:
9½ miles

Starting point:
The car park of the Talbot pub on the B4197 road (with permission) – GR 733561 – or across the river just off the A44 at GR 732559

Maps: OS Explorer 204 Worcester and Droitwich Spa; OS Landranger 150 Worcester and The Malverns, just extending onto OS Landranger 149 Hereford

How to get there: *From the A44 Worcester to Leominster road, turn onto the B4197 Knightwick to Martley road. The pub will be found on the left-hand side, opposite the church.*

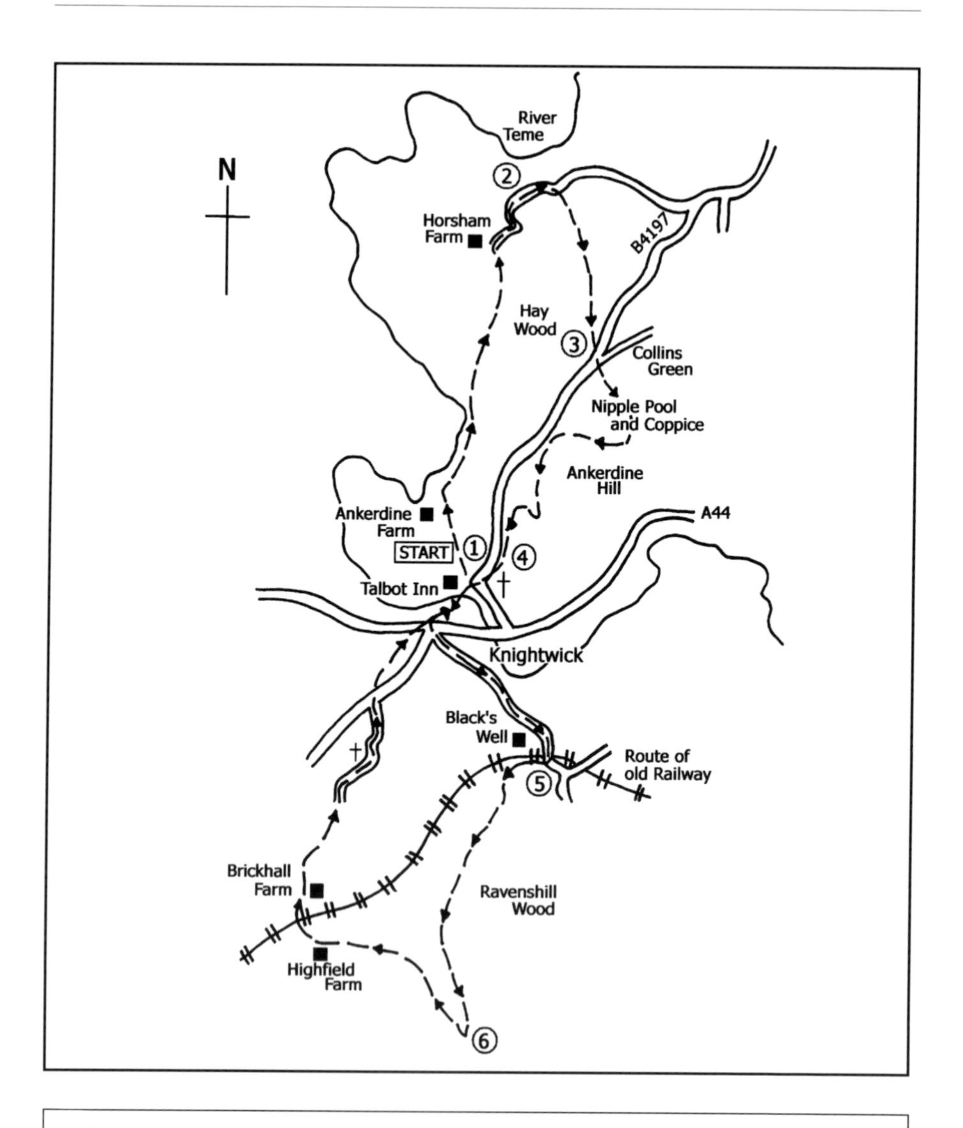

This undulating walk through hops and fruit territory, with fields of pasture and woodlands on some of the hills, crosses some of the county's loveliest, yet less well-known, scenery. The two steep sections afford excellent views, with new landscapes opening up all the time.

The Talbot at Knightwick dates from the 14th century, when it was a coaching inn located at the crossing point of the river, which was formerly a ford. For a long time, it was a farm which brewed beer, as so many old farmhouses did, and now is a thriving family-owned pub with its own Teme Valley Brewery at the rear. The enlarged buildings of the modernised pub also offer bed and breakfast.

The pub offers *an outstanding menu using homegrown or locally produced fruit, vegetables, game and meat. The excellent beers (called This, That or T'Other) are brewed here using local hops.*
Telephone: 01886 821235 (www.the-talbot.co.uk).

① Walk from the surfaced drive alongside the pub, passing between a hop yard on the left and young trees on the right. Already, good views can be enjoyed, notably to Ankerdine up to our right. Pass straight through the farmyard of **Ankerdine Farm** noting the fine house on the left and the towers of the former oasthouses. Once past the buildings the track bends right across open fields with the **River Teme** to the left – and notices emphasising that fishing is 'Private'. The path drifts very close to the river but here we bend right over a stile and onto the stony track across flat and open fields towards **Horsham Farm**. Go over a stile just to the left of the buildings and pass through a farmyard, which can be muddy after wet weather. Veer slightly right to another stile to leave the farmyard and follow the farm driveway out to the narrow road. Pass a ruined building on the right and begin to climb. At the top of the slope are a few houses including an old oasthouse. Turn right just before the first house on the right – at **Hill Top**. ($1\frac{3}{4}$ miles)

② Go over a stile and stay close to the fence on the left. When it bends further to the left, head slightly right and steeply downhill to a gap in the hedge at the bottom, with a small pond to the left. Once through this gap, footpaths go left and right – we take the left option and after a further 30 yards the path divides and we take the right fork. Cross a stile and footbridge and go straight ahead, with **Old House Farm** up on the slope to the left. Climb up to a wooden stile, where there is choice of paths, and continue straight ahead across a rough field, with trees, bracken and a carpet of wildflowers, especially wood anemones in season. Climb on up and reach a telegraph pole at a cross paths. Keep ahead to pass another telegraph pole and then bend left to walk close to the fence, with **Hay Wood** on the right. Reach a stile by a gate, and beyond here pass between two houses and reach the road at **Collins Green**. (3/4 mile)

③ Turn right along the road, pass the narrow road coming in from the left and then turn left down a driveway with a footpath sign. Walk to the right of the house and go on through a metal gate and then steeply down towards the right margin of this field and the edge of the wood – **Nipple Coppice**. Stay near the fence and the edge of the wood, noting the small lake **Nipple Pool**. Cross over the tiny stream and, at a small gate, turn right to enter the woods, following the clear path. This is a wonderful woodland area for wildflowers and birds especially in the spring. After about 200 yards reach a T-junction, where we turn right. We are now on the **Worcestershire Way** with its logo of the pear. Climb quite steeply and reach a patch of fir trees just before the edge of the wood. At a stile, leave the woods and walk on up across the field to a wooden kissing gate to the left of **Tower Cottage**, the house with the tower, which provides wonderful views across towards Worcester. After about 15 yards and before reaching the road, turn left along a stony track – the Worcestershire Way. Pass a picnic spot and keep ahead, beyond a house on the left, then a seat on the right and a house on the right. The driveway ends here, to become a footpath, and after a few yards the Worcestershire Way turns sharp right and begins to descend through the woods, rich in ramsons and many spring flowers. Go down a few steps at first, and once beyond the house on the right, the path divides and we fork left to a T-junction where we go left, descending to reach a few steps and the road. Turn left here to walk

THE TALBOT AT KNIGHTWICK.

down to the pub, passing the **Old School House** on the right.
(1¾ miles)

On the left is the small St Mary's church, built in 1856. (By the entrance is a flood mark showing the height reached by the Teme on 14th May 1886.)

④ Back at the **Talbot**, take the footbridge across the **River Teme**.

Here the river is flowing through the Knightsford Gap – created when melting ice at the end of the Ice Age enlarged the river.

Walk past the doctor's surgery, then cross the main road (A44), following the sign for the **Worcestershire Way**. Once across the main road, the narrow road divides and we take the left fork signed to **Lulsley** and **Alfrick**. Soon begin to climb, passing **Black's Well** on the right. Opposite this house, in the rock wall is a mass of wall pennywort, an amazing plant which seems to survive without soil. Just beyond the point where the old railway line from Worcester to Bromyard once crossed over this road, turn right along a track signed as a bridleway and the **Worcestershire Way**. (1 mile)

⑤ Pass a very smart house, and climb fairly steeply up into the woods to **Wildgoose Cottage**. Reach a sunken section of track before a metal gate and a small open field. We level off here to walk along the ridge, which consists of a series of hills stretching north to south, and generally referred to as the Suckley Hills.

The top of this ridge is mostly covered by woodland some of which is very ancient. Many rotting branches help to provide a wonderful home for a variety of wildlife and support many bunches of mistletoe.

Pass through a small wood and on to a gate and then along an open field, which slopes down to the left. Reach a gate, and just to the left are large barns with a farmhouse beyond. Keep straight ahead across the next short field, with a wood on the right. Pass through two gates and then we have woods on the left, with open views to the right. At the end of this field we reach two gates and continue through small woods – note several linear hollows near here, the remnants of old pits. Just before the open field on the right, notice the simple wooden seat between two tree trunks on the right. Keep straight ahead for 250 yards to reach a stile on the right. We are now on **Rounds Hill**, and beyond a house on the left is **Ravenshill Wood**, managed by the Worcestershire Wildlife Trust.
(1¾ miles)

Ravenshill Wood extends to over 20 hectares and is part of the ancient Wyre Forest. It was mostly felled in 1929 and some planting of conifers took place after that. Modern management includes coppicing and clearing or felling to create a variety of habitats for wildlife.

⑥ Go over the stile, and then diagonally right across the field to the far left corner. Pass through a gap in the hedge and keep straight ahead, descending with a hedge on the left, and at the bottom of this field go through an old gate and turn left to stay close to the hedge. This leads to a stile in the corner, and a narrow track between hedges. Arrive at the duck pond at **Highfields Farm** and a small group of bungalows. The farm buildings contain the towers of former oasthouses, a relic of the hop-growing days in this area. Once beyond the buildings, turn right along the track to **Brickhall Farm**, crossing over the route of the abandoned railway line. Pass the horses' heads gateposts and then another duck pond to walk through a farmyard. A metal gate is our way ahead along the track, described as a 'Public road available for wheeled vehicles'. Stay close to the hedge on the left and then bend right, still close to the field boundary. Continue through the gate and along the track. Pass a derelict house and then a couple of other houses before reaching the delightful **Knightwick** chapel, with farm buildings behind it.

Built in 1879, on the site of a medieval chapel, it is still in use, but only as a cemetery chapel, having been replaced as the local church by the 1856 church at Kingsford Bridge.

The road leads onto a major road and straight across here is a stile with the logo of the **Three Choirs Way** and the quote 'Blessed is the eye between Severn and Wye'. Go over the stile and turn right to follow the direction of the arrow. At the end of the field, fork slightly left through an old orchard to a stile and the main road. Turn right here, passing the Knightwick Butcher and the doctor's surgery to cross the footbridge and return to the **Talbot** once again. (2½ miles)

Date walk completed:

Walk 9

WORCESTER TO POWICK

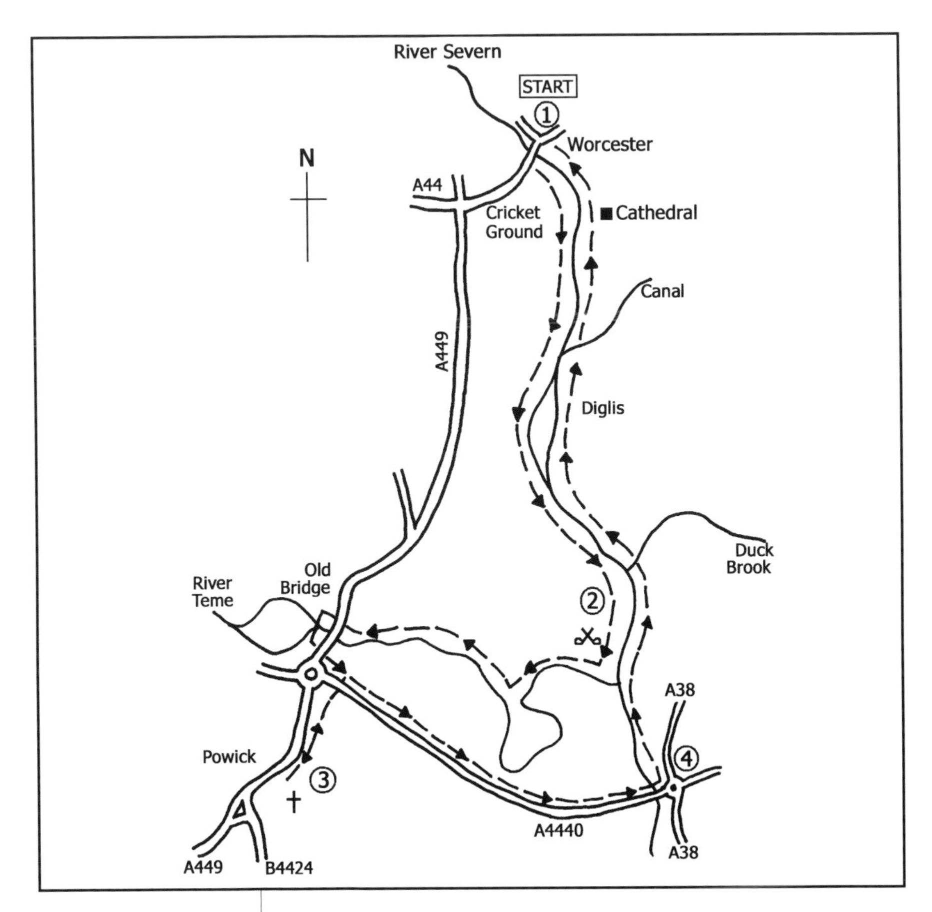

Distance:
$8\frac{1}{2}$ miles

Starting point:
The western end of the river bridge in the centre of Worcester. GR 846547

Maps: OS Explorer 204 Worcester and Droitwich Spa; OS Landranger 150 Worcester and the Malverns

How to get there: *Several main roads lead into the centre of Worcester and there are car parks clearly signed on the east side of the river. Major car parks will be found near the large railway viaduct or alongside the racecourse and Swan Theatre. From any of these car parks it is a short walk to the river bridge and the start of the walk.*

POWICK POWER STATION STANDS NEAR THE OLD BRIDGE.

This is a colourful riverside walk as we follow the willow-fringed banks of the Severn and the Teme, in the company of birds and boats – as well as fishermen. Outstanding architectural and historical interest is provided by the cathedral; Diglis Lock, with its long association with river and canal navigation; and the chimney and old bridge at Powick. Sites of battles in the English Civil War are also visited on this circuit.

The Red Lion at Powick is close to the village church and is the local pub as well as an eating place for visitors. It sits on what was the site of a hospital used to tend the injured during the Battle of Worcester 1651. Recently renovated, it still contains original old beams. The small terrace at the front and the floral displays and hanging baskets make for a colourful setting.

You can enjoy *either a quick snack of sandwiches, a ploughman's, or a full meal. Specialities include fish and vegetarian choices and there are daily extras on the blackboard, as well as tempting traditional English puddings. A good choice of beer will quench any thirst, and the interesting selection of wines includes their own house label. Food is served daily from 12 noon to 2.30 pm and 6 pm to 9.30 pm. Telephone: 01905 830203.*

A second choice of pub is the **Ketch Inn** *on the A38. With long opening hours (food served from 12 noon until 10 pm) and large menu, this popular pub is much used by passing motorists as well as holidaymakers from the adjacent caravan site. Telephone: 01905 821894.*

① Begin at the bridge over the river in **Worcester**, and walk down the right bank (the west side) from the bridge.

Note a plaque on the wall, with a drawing of a trow and the words: 'Up to the mid 19th century this river was the main commercial artery of the West Midlands linking to the sea at Bristol'. The Severn trow was one of the vessels used, typified by its open hold, flat bottom and D-shaped stern.

Pass through a gate and walk along the riverbank, on a dry gravelled path, with numerous seats, and lined with daffodils in spring. Across on the left are old warehouses lining the riverbank, with the spire of **St Andrew's** church and then the cathedral standing at the top of the river valley wall. On the right is the Worcestershire County Cricket ground, then the old boathouse and the playing fields of the **Kings School**. Swans, ducks and gulls are numerous, all expecting to be fed, and this stretch of the river is designated a swan sanctuary. We reach an information board where a kissing gate leads right into the **Chapter Meadows**, but we keep straight ahead along the riverbank.

The Chapter Meadows are now owned by the Duckworth Worcestershire Trust for the people of Worcester – to safeguard the landscape, wildlife and this area of historical importance. The meadows have been cut for hay ever since Roman times. Once the hay has been cut, the land is used for grazing, which helps to preserve the wildlife.

As we move on towards the notice for the weir and the lock, we can see workshops and then the lock entry to **Diglis Basin** across on the other bank. Pass the sewage works, and then the weir, below which there are likely to be fishermen. The main surfaced path turns right to Weir Lane and Bromwich Road, but we keep straight ahead signed to **Powick Bridge**. Go over the stile and continue along the riverbank. Notice the remarkable view looking back, over the lock gates, old industrial debris and the wonderful tower of the cathedral in the background. After two fields, as the river begins to bend round to the right, notice a few houses across the river, perched on top of the valley wall, with good views to the west. Go through a gap into the next field. This was the site of heavy fighting in the Battle of Worcester in 1651, at the close of the Civil War. (2 miles)

THE RED LION AT POWICK.

② We now reach the confluence of the Severn and Teme. Looking downstream is the modern road bridge (Carrington Bridge) over the Severn near to the Ketch. But we turn right, with the **River Teme** on our left side. The **Powick** chimney soon comes into view as we follow the riverbank, passing over a stile, and continuing along the next field to a stile. Do not bend left to follow a large meander, but turn right and cut across the field for about 30 yards to reach the river again. Then turn right to continue walking upstream with the river on the left. The riverside path leads us to the huge sandstone blocks of the tunnel beneath the main A449 road. Continue along the margin of another field to a stile and then turn left onto the old 15th-century **Powick bridge**.

A plaque on a block of Aberdeen granite states: 'In memory of thousands of Scots Highland and Lowland, who fought here far from home so well and so bravely against insuperable odds and gave their lives in devoted loyalty to each other and their leaders. Battle of Worcester 3.9.1651. Unveiled by Tam Dalyell M.P. 2.9.2001'.

Turn left and pass over the old Powick bridge with the converted mill and chimney (part of a hydro electric power station built in 1894 – the first in Britain) to the right. Once across the bridge, turn left over a small stile adjacent to which is another memorial stone and plaque.

This contains the words: 'Powick Bridge. River Teme. During the English Civil Wars between Royalists and Parliamentarians the first skirmish on 23.9.1642 and the last major battle on 3.9.1651 took place on or near this historic bridge. Erected by Powick Parish Council September 1992'.

Cross the small field towards another sandstone tunnel, to the right of the 1837 road bridge. Pass beneath the main road, and turn right. If you are not visiting the pub in **Powick**, head towards the right side of this large field, and walk parallel to the long straight road (the A4440), which is always busy. Alternatively, go over the ladder stile about 20 yards to the right of the tunnel and turn left to follow the main road past the large traffic island and straight on towards Malvern and Ledbury, on the A449. Head towards the church tower, seen straight ahead, to reach the **Red Lion**.
(2 miles)

③ From the pub, visit the church if you have time (bullet holes from the Civil War can be seen in the church wall), and then walk back along the road to the large traffic island. Cross over and turn right to follow the path just inside the field – parallel to the long, straight, main road. The path stays close to the main road, for just over a mile to the **Carrington Bridge** over the River Severn. Before reaching the bridge, pass beneath the road and up on to the bridge on the other side of the road. Cross the bridge, and turn right. Here is a signpost to the riverside path for our onward walk. Also, on the raised platform is a viewpoint with a plan of the Battle site. In addition to the site of the battle, the **Ketch Inn** can be seen. If calling at the inn, walk to this pub before proceeding down to the riverbank. (2 miles)

④ From the viewpoint, follow the sign for the **Severn Way**, with its logo of a trow, as though to pass beneath the main road. We turn sharp left down the slope through the trees, however, to approach the riverbank, and at the level grassy path turn sharp right to walk upstream. The river is on the left, and the caravan park is to the right. At the end of the caravans is a line of conifers and we pass on the left of these, down a few steps, to continue northwards along the riverside path. We soon reach the confluence with the Teme, and then pass a water extraction plant seen earlier from the other bank. A small reservoir is behind the iron fence on the right. The path is clear and well worn, and we soon reach the National River Authority and Severn Way signs where the main path turns right, away from the riverbank. Walk through the woods, and the path leads to a wooden footbridge crossing **Duck Brook** and beyond this turn left to reach the riverside path again.

Here we continue walking upstream, through rich and lush vegetation. Continue alongside the Severn and reach the large warehouses to our right, part of the Diglis Industrial Estate – now less important than in the past as a result of loss of barge traffic along the river. Sand martins may be seen hunting over the river in this section, as we approach **Diglis Locks** and walk along a short stretch of road. As this bends right we keep ahead over a footbridge, and along a high and embanked riverside to reach a swing bridge and the lock for entry to the Diglis Marina and the Worcester-Birmingham Canal, where a signpost tells us the waterway mileage to Birmingham is 30, with 58 locks.

The cathedral is now straight ahead, as we pass a row of cottages, then the Diglis Hotel and Kings School boathouse. A ferry is situated here, and it still functions on summer weekends. But we walk on along the broad surfaced bank, lined with trees, passing the **Water Gate** entry to the cathedral, where heights of floods are recorded on the wall. Once beyond the cathedral, views open up to the technical college at the top of the slope to the right, and the graceful spire of **St Andrew's** church, and then the modernised warehouses, as we reach the main road bridge crossing the Severn – and our starting point. (2½ miles)

Date walk completed:

INKBERROW TO ROUS LENCH

THE OLD BULL IN INKBERROW IS A GRADE II LISTED BUILDING.

Distance:
8½ miles

Starting point:
The pub car park at Inkberrow. GR 015573

An **alternative starting point** *could be in Rous Lench at point number 3. This would provide a mid-walk stopping point for food at the Old Bull.*

Maps: OS Explorer 205 Stratford-upon-Avon and Evesham; OS Landranger 150 Worcester and The Malverns

How to get there: *The starting point in Inkberrow is reached along the A422 from Worcester to Alcester. If coming from Worcester, turn right for 30-40 yards off this main road towards the church and the Old Bull. Parking is available along the narrow road, or at the pub (with permission).*

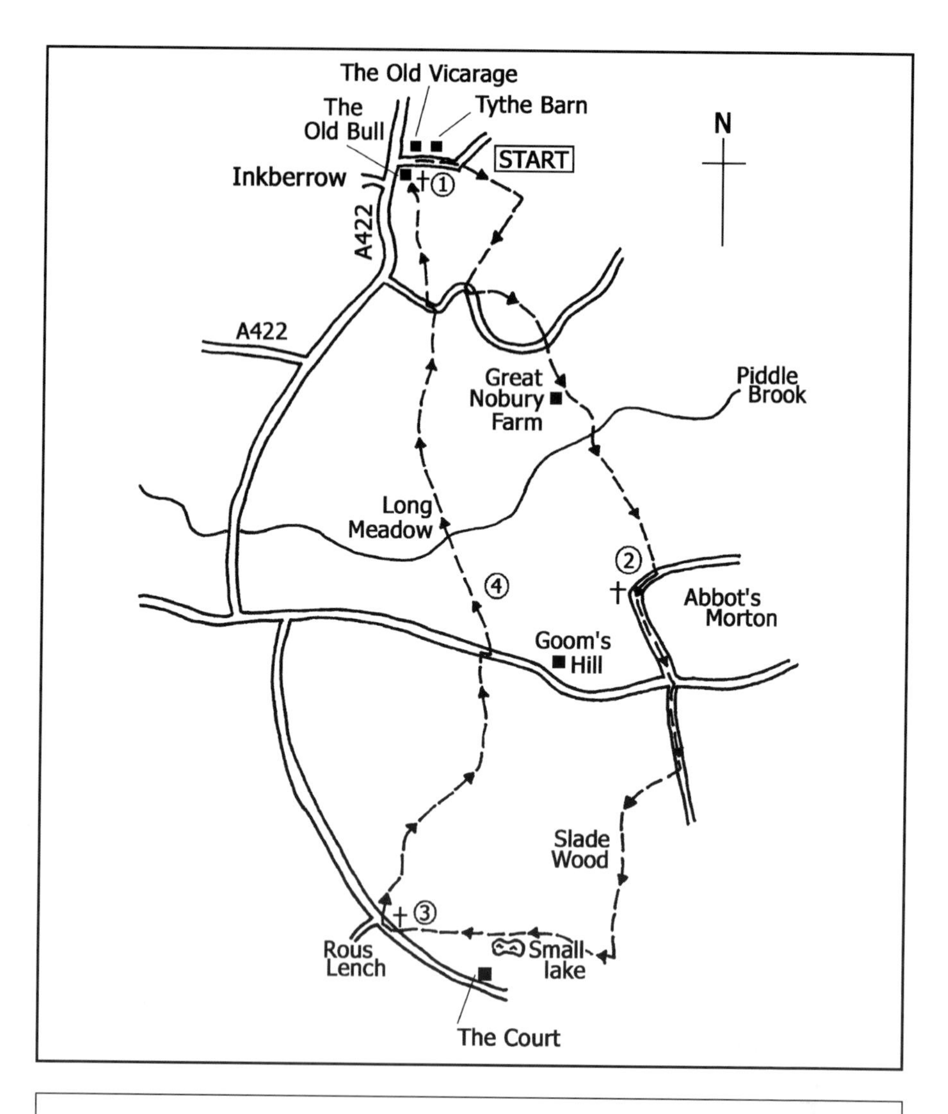

Three attractive villages and beautiful rich farmland are to be seen on this circuit, as well as a nature reserve. Old black and white buildings, magnificent farmhouses and three churches provide interest – as well as a thatched postbox. Peace and quiet adds to the enjoyment as we stroll round the east Worcestershire countryside.

The Old Bull has been a pub since at least 1750 and is a Grade II listed building. Legend suggests that it was a pub in the time of Shakespeare who is thought to have visited here on his way from Stratford to Worcester to obtain his marriage bond. It is a bustling pub, serving regulars as well as passing motorists and it welcomes walkers. Used as the basis of the pub in the Archers radio programme, it is noted for its Ambridge memorabilia, with a family tree of the Archer family and a map of the Ambridge countryside. Log fires are a feature in winter.

A very tasty menu *of main meals is available, with fresh home-cooking and a selection of baguettes and jacket potatoes. Friday night is fish or sausage supper night, with cod and chips served in newspaper at bargain prices. No food is served on Monday. Telephone: 01386 792428.*

The Walk

① From the **Old Bull**, walk along the narrow road passing the converted Tythe Barn, and **Old Vicarage** on the left.

Charles I slept here (the Old Vicarage) on 10th May 1645, on his way to the Battle of Naseby. On the right is the church of St Peter. A Saxon church and an abbey existed in Inkberrow about 700 AD, but the present church dates from the 12th or 13th century, and was much restored in 1840. The north door is the oldest remaining feature and is 13th century. The north chapel contains remnants of a 15th-century window and the massive font is Norman, dating from about 1200 AD. The altar tomb in white marble is a memorial to John Savage who lived in the manor of Edgioke nearby. The three small figures on the canopy represent Time, Hope and Faith. On the outer wall of the south transept is a 'mass clock', a semi circular sundial scratched on the wall.

Go down the hill, with **Millennium Green** on the left and continue ahead as far as the left bend. Take the stony track straight ahead, signed to **Cladswell**, and climb the slight hill. At the end of the field, go over the stile and turn right to walk alongside the hedge, to a stile by a metal gate. Follow the bridleway between a fence and hedge. This leads through to a narrow road, where we turn left for 20 yards as we pass a house, then turn left signed to Nobury. Climb up the left side of the field. At the top of the slope keep straight ahead, along the left side of the hedge. When the hedge bends left, we go right over a stile and straight across the middle of the field (it may be advisable to walk round the edge of this field if going becomes difficult). At the narrow road, continue straight across along the drive towards **Great Nobury**, signed to **Abbots Morton**. After 200 yards, as the drive begins to rise slightly, look for the footpath to the left. Pass through a few trees, over a stile and along the left margin of the field. Climbing slightly, with Great Nobury over to our right, keep straight ahead and descend to the footbridge over **Piddle Brook**. Turn right for a few yards, through the gate and then left alongside the hedge. Half way along this field margin, use the stile to move to the other side of the hedge, but keep straight ahead. Reach another stile and go ahead along the right margin of the field to join a track leading to the houses and the road in **Abbots Morton**. Turn right here and walk through this delightful village, much of which looks as it must have done a hundred years ago. (2¾ miles)

THE THATCHED POST BOX IN ABBOTS MORTON.

Abbots Morton is a small isolated village, with several black and white houses and attractive old cottages. The sandstone church of St Peter is of Saxon origin but was rebuilt by Normans in the 12th century. The font is Norman, the lichen-covered tower has a 14th-century window, and a window in the north transept is from the 15th century. Note also the display of ancient clappers.

② The road turns left by an unusual thatched post box, alongside a thatched house, and there is a seat here if you feel ready for a refreshment break. Straight ahead is the church and it is well worth a short detour. Our walk continues along the narrow road southwards from the church, between hedges containing wild apple trees and many fruits and berries in the autumn. Reach the crossroads and go straight ahead passing the 'No Through Road' sign. After a quarter of a mile, and just beyond a large modernised barn in the midst of lovely gardens, turn right at the bridleway sign. About 80 yards along the track, go left through a gate and turn immediately right on the path which leads to a small gate and entry to **Slade Wood**. A few yards into the wood, turn left along a clear path. A steady climb leads up through the woods and once on the level, the path soon divides and we fork left – the major path. A large field can be seen sloping down to our left, as we approach the end of the wood which we leave through a small gate. The path leads alongside a hedge on the left and young trees to the right, to reach a crosspath.

Turn right here towards the green barn and, after a few yards, go right again through the large metal gate. Walk up the broad grassy track between young trees for about 100 yards to a stile by a gate. Continue ahead alongside the hedge on the left to a stile and on along the left side of the next field. Reach a stile in the end hedge and, once over this, turn left to walk in a westerly direction towards the line of fir trees at the far side of this large field. The path should cross through this field but, if it is not clear, stay close to the left margin passing near the tall tower in the grounds of **The Court**. Go over a stile, through the line of trees, and on towards a marker post in the middle of the field. **The Court** is on the left, but probably not visible through the trees. Descend quite sharply to a stile, cross a small field to another stile and walk alongside the wire fence with an artificial lake to the left. As the wire fence round the pond and paddock bends left, near a grand Wellingtonia tree, keep straight ahead across the large parkland field towards the hedge and trees ahead. Approaching this hedge aim into the right corner, where an iron kissing gate leads along a short avenue of yew trees into the churchyard of **St Peter** at **Rous Lench**. (2½ miles)

The grey sandstone church of St Peter dates from Norman times. Above the south doorway is a relief of Christ, seated and blessing, probably from 1140. Paintings and monuments, including a memorial to Edward Rous who died in 1611, are amongst other items of interest. The timber-framed cottages around the green help to make this a very attractive village.

③ Leave the churchyard onto the road and turn right for a few yards. Opposite the unusual VR post box and the village green is a footpath sign, pointing along the driveway to the left of a yellow walled house. Walk along the left margin of the garden and a small paddock, passing a green shed, to reach a stile. Head slightly diagonally across the middle of the next field, aiming towards the left corner of the wood. Pass over a stile by an iron gate, and veer slightly right towards the fence as we cross the next field towards two iron gates. Continue through the left gate to the grassy track along the right margin of the next two fields. Bend right near the end of the second field, to go on through a gate and turn immediately left to stay close to a hedge and ditch. A few isolated oak trees are dotted around in these fertile fields of cereals. Keep straight ahead through three fields to reach the road. Turn right for 20 yards towards **Gooms Hill Farm**. (1½ miles)

④ Just before the farm, turn left over a stile to pass to the left of the farm buildings. After the small paddocks, keep ahead along the left margin of a larger field, to twin stiles and straight on across the middle of the next field. Then cross the **Piddle** by a stiled footbridge and reach the board providing information about the **Long Meadow Nature Reserve**.

The large hay meadow to our left is affected by winter flooding but coloured by cowslips, green winged orchids and many other flowers in spring and early summer. Badgers and marbled white butterflies are amongst the other local attractions. Hay is cut in July and then the land is used for grazing.

Continue ahead up the short, steep, wooded slope, over the stile (with a badger gate alongside) and straight across the next field. Go on over the top of a slight rise to the next stile. Go left, then right, along the margin of the next field, and into another field with the hedge now on the right. **Inkberrow** church tower and village are now in sight. Go on over the stile and along the right margin of the field to another stile and out on to the road. Turn left for 30 yards and then right to walk between modern houses. When the road bends left, turn right up a few stone steps and cross three small meadows and pass the pond to enter the churchyard. The pub is just a few yards along the road to the right. (1¾ miles)

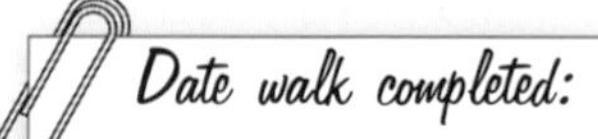

Walk 11

HANBURY

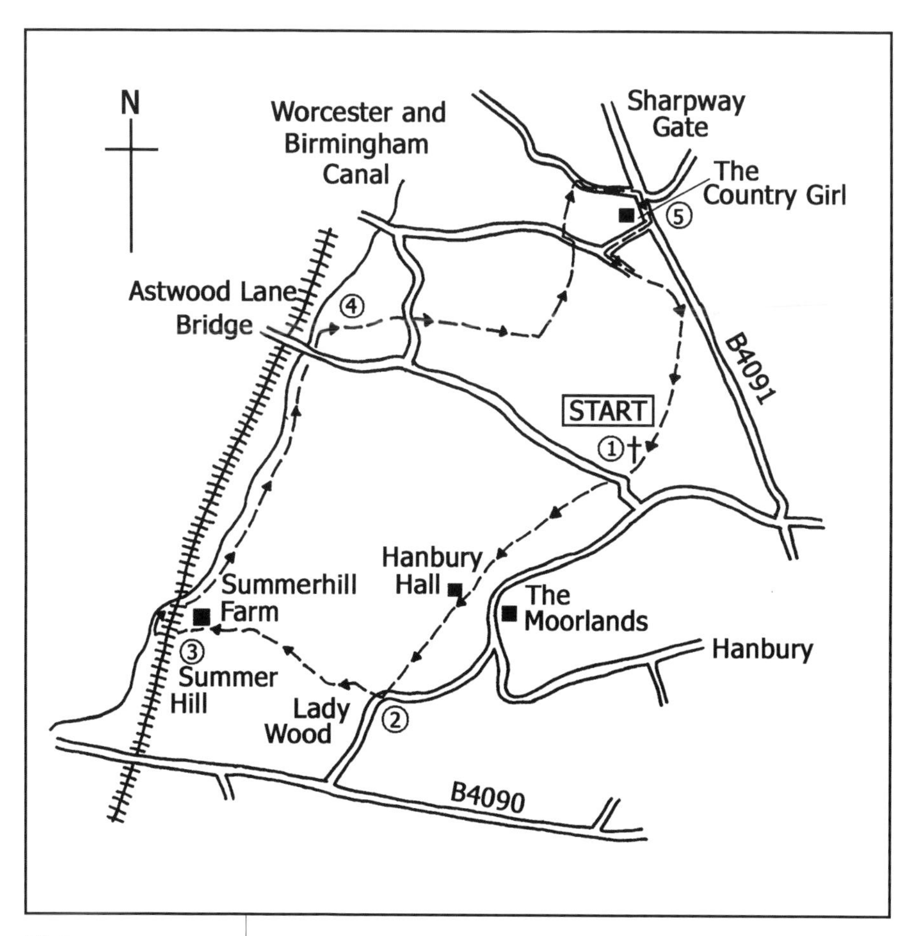

Distance:
7¾ miles

Starting point:
Hanbury church. GR 954644

Maps: OS Explorer 204 Worcester and Droitwich Spa; OS Landranger 150 Worcester and The Malverns

How to get there: *The M5 junction 5 and the A38 will lead into Droitwich, and from here take the B4090 signed to Hanbury and Feckenham. Some 3 miles along here, fork left on the narrow road signed to Hanbury Hall and Hanbury church.*

THE WALK CROSSES THE PARKLAND OF HANBURY HALL.

This historical circuit starts from medieval St Mary's church and crosses the parkland of Hanbury Hall (completed in 1701). Next we follow the towpath of the 18th-century Worcester-Birmingham canal, a relic of former industry but now only used by narrowboats. Then we continue over undulating countryside to an inviting pub and return to the starting point by passing through one of Worcestershire's most popular nature reserves, with trees several hundred years old.

The village of Hanbury is located near the junction of the B4090 and B4091, and stretches northwards towards the Jinny Ring Craft Centre, housed in restored barns alongside the 17th-century farmhouse. Crafts to be seen here include glassblowing and jewellery making, and there are shops and a café, as well as wonderful views to the Malvern Hills.

The Country Girl at Sharpway Gate, near Stoke Prior, has a spacious interior, a large outside area for use in the summer and a large car park, too.

It is open for food *every lunch time, with a choice of jacket potatoes and baguettes as well as full-scale meals. Home-made steak and ale pie was a tasty and filling dish on my last visit, and the Wye Valley ale will refresh any walkers. Telephone: 01527 821790.*

The Walk

① From the church, walk down the driveway to reach a division in the roads – with a house on the right. Go ahead across the road and through the wooden kissing gate into the parkland of **Hanbury Hall**. Follow the path across the large field, with views of the motorway ahead in the distance. Reach a stile by a large wooden gate, and walk on between lines of oak trees to another stile by a gate. Continue along more of the tree-lined avenue, and just before reaching a driveway, the path divides and we take the left fork. Go over a stile and across a driveway (for staff and trade) and pass to the left of a small pool. Note the large decorated house – the **Moorlands** – over to the left. Reach another stile by a gate and to our left is the car park for visitors to Hanbury Hall.

The red-brick, William and Mary-style house was completed in 1701 by Thomas Vernon, whose descendants lived here until 1962. Famous for its staircase and painted ceilings, the house is surrounded by 8 hectares of gardens, with a recreated 18th-century crown bowling green, and 160 hectares of parkland. As we walk past, we can see the Orangery and the Moorish gazebos but the Hall is well worth a visit. Managed by the National Trust, it is open from Easter until the end of October.

Cross over the driveway, which leads through the iron gates to the main entrance of the imposing Hall, to reach another stile with the ha-ha to our right. As the ha-ha and boundary wall bend to our right, we keep straight ahead across a huge field. Pass to the left of a small pond and aim towards the left end of a line of trees where another pond is on the right. Reach a stile by the gate, and go over towards the road. (1½ miles)

② Once beyond the stile, turn immediately right, over another stile to pass to the side of the pool, and through a small field to reach a stile. Turn right along the field margin, with woods to our right. At the end of this field, the path divides but we turn left along the field margin, with a hedge to our right. Look for the stiled footbridge on our right and, once over here, head across the next field to the corner of **Lady Wood** and follow the arrow ahead. Gradually diverge further away from the woodland, and climb steadily up **Summer Hill** to reach a metal gate at the far end of this field. From here, go on down the slope along a sunken track heading towards the buildings of **Summerhill Farm**. Do not go along the drive towards the buildings but, instead, turn left along the farm drive for a few yards and then right through a metal gate. Follow the footpath leading to the bridge over the railway which can be clearly seen ahead. Cross over the railway with care and then go through one more field to reach the canal. (1¼ miles)

③ Climb the stile to the left of the canal bridge in order to gain access to the towpath and turn right. Follow the canal and pass beneath the railway line (bridge 37) and then a farm bridge (38) for **Summerhill Farm**. Continue along the towpath, with views to **Hanbury church** on its hill over to the right, and the tall masts of the **Wychbold** radio station ahead to our left. After passing **Astwood Bottom Lock**, we soon arrive at the **Astwood Lane** road bridge (bridge 40). (1½ miles)

④ We pass beneath the road bridge to reach the lock and a cottage. Continue along the towpath for 100 yards and then turn right over a stile to walk along the right margin of the field. The next section of the walk involves numerous fields and also numerous stiles. Reach twin stiles and a footbridge and keep ahead along the field margin to another stile, and then diagonally across the next field to a stile and gate. Turn right along the road for a few yards and then go left along the field margin. At the end of the large field go over a stile to a grassy track, straight across to another stile, beyond which turn left over stiles and a footbridge. Head diagonally right across the next field to a stile in the hedge. Note the Wychbold masts over to the left, and long views to **Abberley Hill**. Go up the field to a gate and continue along the right

THE COUNTRY GIRL AT SHARPWAY GATE, NEAR STOKE PRIOR.

side of the next field to another gate. Stay near the right margin of the next field (farm buildings up to the right) to a stile in the right corner and out onto the road. Turn left along the road for 100 yards and then go right over the stile and stay close to the right margin. Reach a double stile and footbridge, then head diagonally left across the next field to a stile and continue along the edge of the next small field to reach a stile and gate, and the road. Turn right, climbing slightly and, at **Hanbury Road**, turn right and after 200 yards, arrive at the **Country Girl**. (2 miles)

⑤ Take the narrow road alongside the pub, and 200 yards along here turn sharp left on **Sharpway Gate** and continue to the end of this cul-de-sac where two footpaths go into the woods.

Piper's Hill Common is one of the most popular of the Worcestershire Wildlife Trust Nature Reserves, covering 15½ hectares on either side of the B4091. Designated as a Site of Special Scientific Interest, the wood contains many ancient beech and sweet chestnut, as well as large oaks which are thought to be more than 300 years old.

As we enter the woods, the left fork goes through to the car park which can be used as an alternative starting point, alongside the B4091. Walk along the right fork into the woods and come to a broader track to pass the right side of a pond. Look out for dragonflies around here. Follow the path which is just inside the right margin of the woods clothing **Piper's Hill**. Emerge onto a track and at the kissing gate beside a large metal gate, the church can be seen at the top of the hill. As we climb up this slope, **Church Coppice** is to our right. Pass through a kissing gate before the final few yards of the climb and the completion of the walk. (1½ miles)

At the top is the prominently located church, on the site of a former Iron Age fort. Panoramic views give a bird's eye view of the countryside. This medieval red sandstone church dates from the 12th century though changes were made in the 18th and 19th centuries.

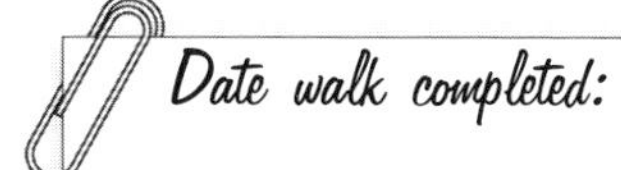

Walk 12

REDDITCH – ARROW VALLEY COUNTRY PARK

THE SAILING CLUB IN ARROW VALLEY COUNTRY PARK.

Distance:
8 miles

Starting point:
The Countryside Centre at Arrow Valley Country Park. GR 065677

Maps: OS Explorer 220 Birmingham, Walsall, Solihull and Redditch; or OS Landranger 150 Worcester, The Malverns and surrounding area

How to get there: *Take the main road A448 from Bromsgrove to Redditch and look for the major crossroads and large island where the A441 crosses the A448. At this point the A448 turns right (to join the A441), but we need to keep straight ahead for a further 1½ miles along what is now called the A4189. Just past Morrisons supermarket on the left, reach a traffic island and turn left off the A4189 along the B4497, Battens Drive. The entrance to Arrow Lake is half a mile along here.*

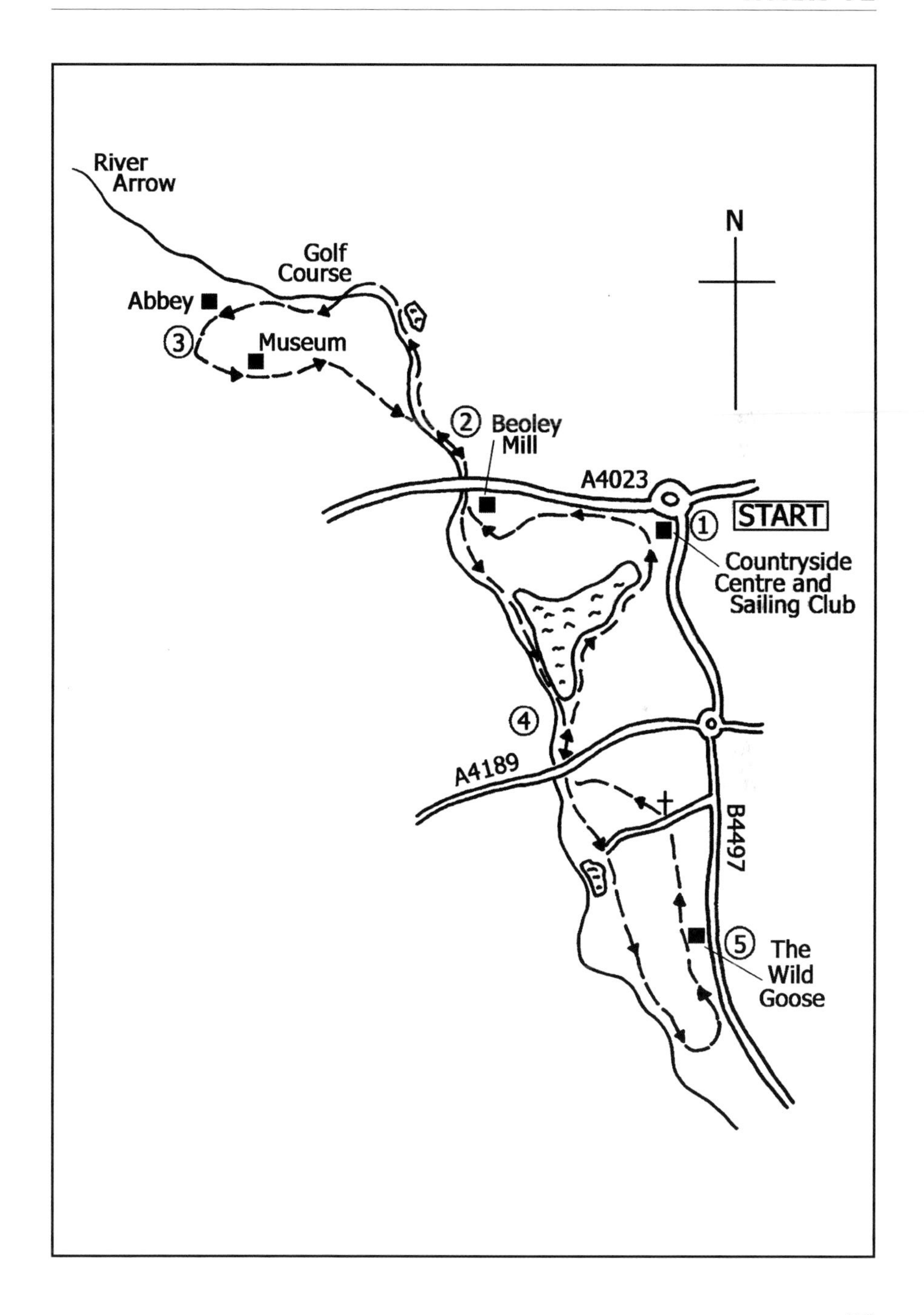
River
Arrow
Golf
Course
Abbey
3
Museum
N
2
Beoley
Mill
A4023
START
1
Countryside
Centre and
Sailing Club
4
A4189
B4497
5
The
Wild
Goose

Redditch was noted in the past for old metal industries, shown and explained in the Forge Mill Needle Museum, and then in more modern times as a Birmingham overspill town. It was designated a New Town in 1964 – hence all the modern housing and numerous roads. In the midst of all this, however, is the Arrow Valley Country Park, for which Redditch should also be noted. Walking, jogging, dog walking, boating, birds, flowers, trees with blossom, pussy willows, catkins in spring – quite a surprise!! This is a true rural landscape in the heart of an urban area, and our gentle walk with only slight gradients, explores much of the park.

The Wild Goose on Wild Goose Lane is a Mitchells & Butlers pub in a modern-style 1970s building. It enjoys a wonderful location on the edge of the country park, adjacent to playing fields and next door to the skateboard park. There is a spacious bar and a separate room for families whilst outside there is a garden and play area as well as access to playing fields.

The pub offers *a good choice of food such as steaks, chicken and bacon with salad, and also baguettes. Telephone: 01527 830951.*

The Walk

① Leave the Countryside Centre alongside the staff car park. Follow the orange arrows for the **Meadows Trail**, which is a surfaced path. Keep ahead across an open grassy patch. Just before the end of this grass, turn left through an iron kissing gate. The path divides at an information board (about WET and the Millennium Wood). Fork left at this notice-board, and then left again at post number 1 to cross an open field.

At the left edge of this field is the Wetland Ecosystem Treatment area which consists of four small ponds, where the waste from the Countryside Centre is treated. Twenty-five species of indigenous wetland plants have been planted, as well as 15,000 willows which will eventually be coppiced and used for basket-making.

As the path bends right, go left across the grass to a few steps and a wooden walkway to a metal kissing gate. We are now entering **Proctor's Barn** wild flower meadow. Turn left to cross this field to reach another metal kissing gate, alongside a larger gate.

Reach a narrow road and turn right, no longer following the Meadows Trail, and soon fork left off this road to walk towards a wooden footbridge. Just before this footbridge, turn right along a surfaced path which is the route of the **Miller's Trail** (maroon arrow) – post number 2. The horse riding trail and the river Arrow are just to our left, with small trees and undergrowth providing wonderful habitat for birds. The former Beoley Paper Mill is to our right. Cross another narrow road within the park and walk beneath the A4023. Cross a small stream and the maroon arrow points us to the left, where the horse trail goes straight ahead. Pass **Miller's Trail** post number 3. (1½ miles)

② The path divides with the left fork going over a footbridge (the route of our return), but we go right here, passing beneath another road. At the T-junction turn left following the maroon arrow. Pass a pond and then two bridges on our right, as we arrive at post number 4. The river is on our left and an old millpond is to the right – the path may be muddy along this section after rain. Reach a footbridge (note the old weir and evidence of an old building) and beyond this our path turns left. A golf course is to the right. Cross another footbridge and then turn right still following the maroon arrow – and here we pass a notice welcoming us to the **Bordesley Abbey Meadows**. We are now on a surfaced gravel path with a small stream to the right. Go right over a footbridge and then immediately left – to reach post number 5 on the **Miller's Trail**. At a cross paths keep straight ahead, passing a narrow lake to the right, a restored monastic fishpond. Behind the iron fence to our right is the site of **Bordesley abbey**.

Part of the abbey church has been uncovered but most of the other remains are under grass. The medieval Cistercian abbey was founded in 1138 and survived until the dissolution by Henry VIII in the 16th century. An exhibition in the visitor centre explains how the 12th-century monks worked and worshipped.

Keep ahead to post number 6 where we go through the gate and across the footbridge. (1¼ miles)

③ Walk past the entrance to the **museum**, inside which can be seen the history of needle making in Victorian times.

The atmosphere of working in those times has been recreated, but the museum also has exhibitions of contemporary textiles, and a small shop. The workshop was the only water-powered needle scouring mill in the world, and much of the original machinery can be seen. The mill was used from 1730-1958, and the water wheel is still run occasionally. For opening times, telephone 01527 62509.

Once past the entrance, turn right at post number 7 and, after about 50 yards, turn left along a narrow path between fences and hedges, and between two pools. Once beyond the pools turn left, following the maroon arrow, with the millpond on the left, and houses on the right. At the end of the pool, turn right alongside the wooden fence (not left through the kissing gate) and reach the gap in the hedge, then turn left and go down hill slightly with the hedge on the left. Pass through another gap and turn right, with the hedge now on the right. We are now in a grassy field and at the end of this field turn right through a metal gate, to leave the **Bordesley Abbey Meadows** and follow the path between hedges. Reach a road, cross straight over and, after a further 30 yards, turn left along a narrower

THE WILD GOOSE PUB AT IPSLEY.

road which leads through to a footpath, with allotments to the right. Go over the footbridge to reach a junction of paths, seen earlier. Fork right here and retrace your steps along the earlier route, as far as the point where there is a wooden footbridge going right, (we had earlier approached from the left). Keep straight ahead here, following the **Miller's Trail**. The **Meadows Trail** joins us, and soon the **Miller's Trail** goes left, but we keep straight ahead (as part of the Meadows, Woodland and Lakeside Walks). The lake is now on our left. Popular for fishing, boating and bird watching, the lake is home to a variety of birds, notably swans, black swans, geese, ducks, great crested grebes, gulls and goosander. Pass post number 3 on the **Lakeside Trail** and, looking across the lake, you can see the sailing club and then the Countryside Centre. At the end of the lake go right, following the sign for the **Woodland Trail**. (2 miles)

④ Once past the end of the lake, the surfaced path divides and we fork right along the **Woodland Trail** – with the River Arrow to our right. Soon pass beneath a road, with a basketball court also sheltering beneath this busy road. Keep straight ahead following the sign pointing to Ipsley church and Matchborough and we soon join a narrow road. This is **Ipsley Church Lane**, which bends left to go to the church, but we keep straight ahead. Pass the **Old Mill House** on the left, and continue southwards. Notice a football pitch through trees to the left, and an old established hedge on the right. Our route bends left, at a point where there is a bridge over the river to our right, and a narrow (and often muddy) path goes straight ahead. Go beneath power lines and the path divides but we keep straight ahead and soon pass a building on the left (formerly the sport changing rooms) and reach a car park. Turn left at the narrow road (about 20 yards before reaching a major road). A few houses are on our right, with hedge and playing fields to the left. The road ends but a footpath keeps straight ahead and leads directly to the **Wild Goose**. (1½ miles)

⑤ From behind the pub, cross the playing field diagonally to the right. Note the iron fence around the imaginative skatepark to the right, and **Ipsley** church tower is also to the right.

The skatepark is open March to October (weather permitting) from 12 noon till 8 pm on Saturday and Sunday and during school holidays, and from 4 pm to 8 pm Monday to Friday. Cost is £1.50 for three hours and all income goes into the running costs and creating new projects. The

skatepark is one of the largest in the UK, and caters for skaters and BMX bikers, and is suitable for beginners and professionals.

Turn right along the far side of the playing field, with trees and shrubs on the left. At the end of the field, just before a hedge, trees and a small pool, bend to the right, still on the edge of the grass. After 100 yards, turn left and head straight across the next field to reach the notice for the entrance to the **Arrow Valley Country Park**. Go straight across the narrow road and into the arboretum. A few yards to the right along the road is **St Peter's** church, Ipsley, which probably dates from the 13th century, though much changed over the centuries. Next door to it is the large building of GKN Corporate Centre. Once in the arboretum, the path immediately divides and we take the right fork and keep straight ahead at the next fork.

Turn left at the next marker post (number 4) and, at a crosspath, turn right and begin to go downhill, with silver birch on the left of this broad path. Near the bottom of this slope keep straight ahead past post number 3 and across the grassy patch heading towards a road bridge – this is Warwick Highway, the A4189. At the main surfaced path, turn right, passing the basketball court beneath the bridge (we are now retracing our steps on the earlier part of the walk). With the river to the left, keep straight ahead to reach point 4 of our walk. Turn right and follow the blue arrow for the **Lakeside Trail** to return to the starting point. (1¾ miles)

Date walk completed:

STOKE HEATH, BROMSGROVE AND TARDEBIGGE

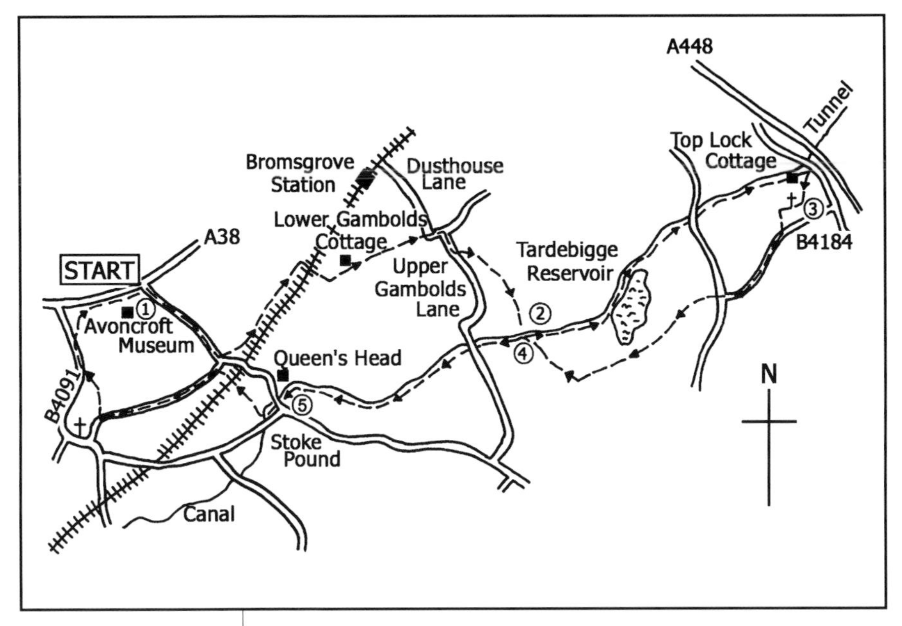

Distance:
$10\frac{3}{4}$ miles

Starting point:
Avoncroft Museum, Stoke Heath, Bromsgrove. GR 953685

Maps: OS Explorer 204, Worcester and Droitwich Spa; or OS Landranger mostly on 139 Birmingham and surrounding area, but just extending on to 150 Worcester area

How to get there: *The museum is located along the A38 bypass road, 2 miles south of Bromsgrove and just 400 yards north of its junction with the B4091. Park in the museum car park or an alternative starting point is at Tardebigge church, GR 996691, beginning the walk at Point 3.*

SOME OF THE MANY LOCKS ON THE WORCESTER-BIRMINGHAM CANAL.

Gently undulating though with a steady climb whilst passing the locks, this walk takes in glorious countryside with long views. Modern developments near Bromsgrove contrast with the historical and industrial past and history of the area as seen along the canal and in the Avoncroft Open Air Museum.

The Queen's Head is located at Stoke Pound bridge, which was built at the same time as the pub – whilst the canal was being dug. Formerly known as the Blacksmith's Arms as it was once the site of a smithy and was also used as a post office for a few years. There is a large car park and a delightful canalside garden.

Bar snacks are available, *as well as a wide range of meals in the large restaurant. Real ales, lagers and cider are on tap.*
Telephone: 01527 877777.

① From **Avoncroft Museum** and Picnic Site, walk along the narrow road towards **Stoke Pound**. Cross over the small brook and continue along **Sugarbrook Lane**. Just before the railway line, turn left on the narrow surfaced footpath. The busy railway line is on the right and an old industrial site to the left.

After nearly half a mile, reach a bridge where we turn right over the railway (Bromsgrove station is along the line looking left) to go over a stile and along the left side of a field. Turn left over a stile by a large iron gate, taking the middle of the choice of three footpaths. The hedge is on the left. At the end of the field, go over a stile by a gate and onto a track with a house (Lower Gambolds Cottage) on the left.

Continue along the track which becomes a narrow surfaced road and, at a major road, turn right along **Dusthouse Lane** signed towards Stoke Cross and Tardebigge. After 100 yards, turn right along **Upper Gambolds Lane**. When this road bends slightly right, go off to the left along a farm track, but when this track turns towards the farm buildings, keep straight ahead along the left margin of the field. At the end of this field, pass through a small gate and along the left margin of the next field.

Climb steadily, with good views back over to Bromsgrove, and walk on through a gap in the hedge along the left edge of the next field. At the end of this field turn left through a gate, along a few yards of footpath to another gate beyond which is the bridge over the canal. Cross to the other side and turn left on the towpath. (3 miles)

The Worcester-Birmingham canal was constructed in the 18th century, mainly to carry coal and salt. Permission to build went through Parliament in 1791 but it was not completed down to Worcester until 1815. The flight of 36 locks from Stoke Pound to Tardebigge is the longest in Britain, and Tardebigge is at the top of 30 locks in the space of 2½ miles.

Altogether the canal has 5 tunnels and 58 locks in 31 miles, and the locks lift boats by more than 400 ft. Top Lock at Tardebigge is the deepest in Britain (14ft). A vertical boatlift had been planned here but tests were unsuccessful and so the lock was built instead.

Above this lock and just before the tunnel, the small settlement of New Wharf was opened in 1811, before the tunnel was completed. Tug Row Cottages and a maintenance yard with

workshops still survive, but in former times there was also a carpenter's shop, a forge, and stables for the horses and donkeys. The tug waited here to tow boats through the tunnel, as there is no towpath.

② Walk steadily uphill now, passing a series of locks. Just beyond a bridleway going right, there is a useful wooden seat, and a few steps which lead up to the **Tardebigge Reservoir**.

Originally dug for clay to line the canal, this lake was then used for water storage to replenish the upper locks. Now noted for its abundant bird life, the lake is also popular with fishermen.

Continue on the towpath, passing a closely packed set of locks (numbers 50-57) to reach **Tylers Lock**, where the old engine house which took water from Tardebigge Reservoir to maintain supplies in the canal, has been converted into a restaurant. Walk on to lock 58, **Top Lock**, with Top Lock Cottage alongside, and then arrive at **New Wharf** and the tunnel.

Above the opening to the tunnel can be seen and heard the traffic on the road. The tunnel is 580 yards in length, cut through red

THE QUEENS HEAD IS DELIGHTFULLY SITUATED BESIDE THE CANAL.

sandstone, and daylight can be seen at the other end.

A few yards before reaching the tunnel, go through the kissing gate on the right and take the footpath leading up towards the church. Climb this slope to the kissing gate and walk into the corner of the car park serving the church and the village school. (2 miles)

St Bartholomew's church is an estate church. The old 12th/13th-century church tower collapsed in 1775, and the present church dates from 1777, with a very tall tower and thin spire (built by Francis Hiorn). Notice the unusual baroque bell stage at the base of the spire. The church was largely rebuilt in the 19th century and many craftsmen from the Plymouth estate (from nearby Hewell Grange) were involved in new woodworking in the chancel. The font dates from 1850 but is Norman in style and, amongst other features of interest, are several of the monuments in the churchyard. Enjoy the wonderful views all around from the lofty site of the church.

③ Proceed from the church, between the graveyard on the right and the school. Just beyond the school, turn left onto the narrow path running alongside the playground and field, to walk through to a kissing gate and the narrow road. Turn right here and follow this road for nearly half a mile, passing the restored buildings of **High House Farm**. Where the road divides, with **London Lane** going right and **High House Lane** going left, keep straight ahead through a large metal gate and along the bridleway. This track leads us past a pond and on towards **Patchetts Farm**. Go through an iron gate, and about 100 yards before reaching the farm, as the track bends right, go left off the track and across a field. At the hedge and fence, where three footpaths are signed, go over the stile and turn right. Walk alongside the hedge, cross the track from the farmyard, pass a large barn and keep ahead through a gate and across the next field – to the right of a telegraph pole. At the end of this field, pass through a few trees and over a footbridge, then follow the left margin of the next field to return to the canal – by bridge 52. Turn left. (2 miles)

④ Walk gently downhill alongside a few of the **Tardebigge** locks numbered 44, 43, 42 and so on. At lock 41 is also a bridge, numbered 51 as bridges have their own series of numbers. A large farm (Stoke Court) is away to our right, as we reach Tardebigge bottom lock, which is the start of the Tardebigge flight. Then we reach the **Queen's Head** on the other side of the canal. (1½ miles)

⑤ Continue along the towpath as far as the next bridge, number 47, where we cross to the other side of the lock, to go over the stile and turn sharp right along the field margin. Follow the fence as it bends to the left, and soon cross over a small stile and continue along the other side of the fence. Reach a stile and proceed along a path between fences and small trees to a stile where we cross the main railway line – taking great care. Beyond the railway line head diagonally right across a small field, to reach a stile and a narrow road. Turn left here for about half a mile and where the road bends sharp left (**Stoke Prior** church is just a few yards further along this road), turn right at the bridleway sign, along a track to pass between houses, including **Bridge House** on the left. The track narrows to a grassy path, and reaches a bridge over the small River Salwarpe. The path bends left and begins to climb, with trees and bushes overhanging from both sides. At the top as the path opens out, notice the views to the windmill in Avoncroft, and we reach a main road B4091. Turn right past the **Epic Bar Brasserie**, and then leave the road to follow the path diagonally right across the cricket field. Cross a narrow road and go straight ahead along a footpath between fences, to reach the main A38 Bromsgrove bypass. Turn right. Soon reach the large sign saying Avoncroft Museum of Historic Buildings (open March to November. Telephone 01527 831886) at the next turning on the right, but look for a short cut along a road blocked by bollards, leading us directly into the **Avoncroft** car park. (2¼ miles)

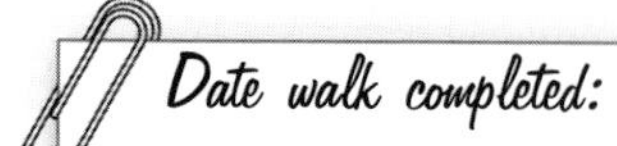

Walk 14

SHRAWLEY WOODS

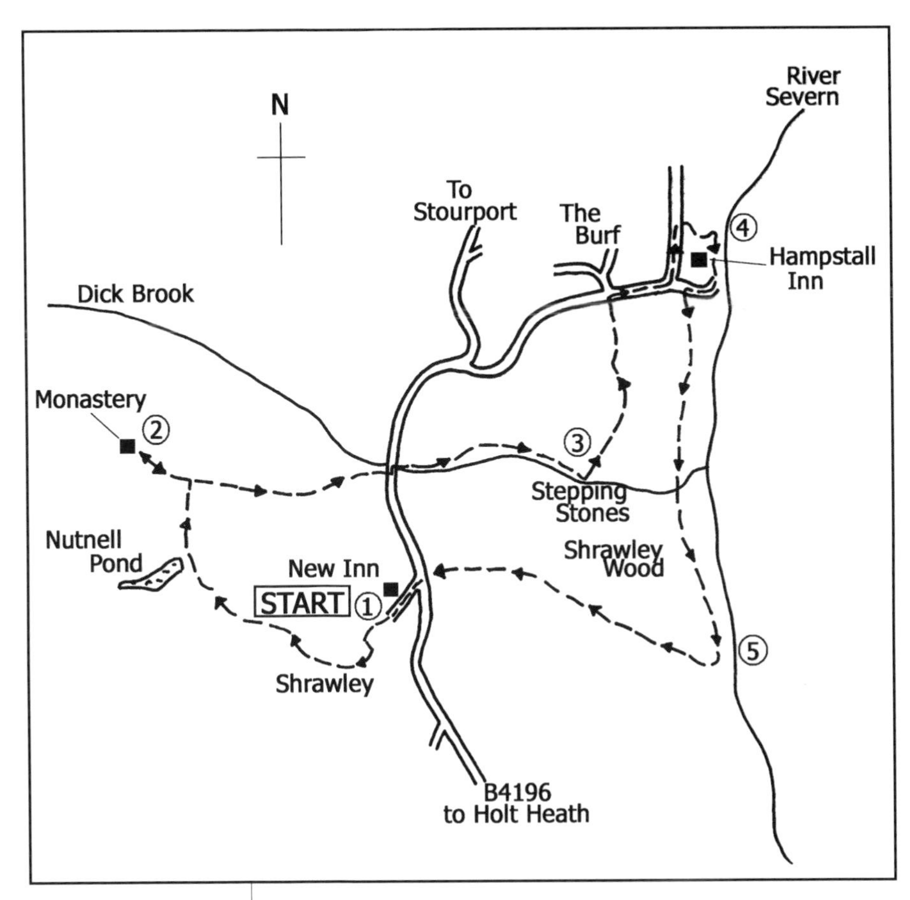

Distance:
$7\frac{1}{2}$ miles

Starting point:
The County Council walkers' car park at the rear of the New Inn. GR 799663

Maps: OS Landranger 150 Worcester, The Malverns and surrounding area; Explorer 204 Worcester and Droitwich Spa

How to get there: *From the A449 Worcester to Kidderminster road, turn west at Ombersley along the A4133. Cross the River Severn and at Holt Heath turn right on the B4196 to Shrawley and Stourport. Nearly 3 miles along this road, reach the New Inn and turn left into the County Council walkers' car park.*

THE STEPPING STONES SEEN AT POINT 4 OF THE WALK.

It is difficult to imagine as we take in the rural scene that this area was once a hive of industry, bustling with workshops and a forge. Our circuit takes us across fields and then follows Dick Brook, partially canalised with locks to improve navigation in the 17th century. We then go through a wood, over more fields and a stretch close to the River Severn before passing through the heart of Shrawley wood. The wood is famous for its small-leaved lime trees, and also for the oaks, some of which were used in the repair of the Houses of Parliament after bomb damage in the Second World War.

The New Inn, in spite of its name, is an old building, having been a butcher's shop and slaughterhouse in the early 19th century. It is open all day and every day, and offers a warm welcome to walkers. Besides the main bar, there is a bar billiards room and a restaurant.

The ample menu *provides a choice of snacks or large-scale meals freshly cooked, and a choice of beers. Specialities include the all-day breakfast and a very popular Sunday lunch. Telephone: 01299 822701.*

The Walk

① Leave the small County Council car park and turn right along **New Inn Lane**. Walk between houses, and just beyond the last house on the right, as the surfaced road ends to become a track, take the next footpath on the left, signed '**Monastery and Goodyear**'. Go through the wooden gate by a metal gate and along the right side of the small field to another wooden kissing gate. Then go right to cross the next field, climbing slightly to a kissing gate, with **Bonefields Farm** 100 yards to the right. Keep straight ahead down the other side to reach an isolated stile, with no hedge or fence, where paths go left and right. To the left is a caravan site down in the hollow, but we turn right along the field margin, to reach another stile. Keep ahead, following the sign to the **monastery**, with the hedge on the right for about 20 yards before the path bends slightly left across the field to reach a gate.
Continue along the right margin of the next field, with a hedge and ditch on the right. Walk alongside a small wood and a deep valley on our right and at the end of the wood, turn right for about 30 yards to a stile. **Abberley Tower** is now visible over to the left, and the **monastery** is on the hilltop ahead. Turn left along the left margin of the next field, passing a path which goes left, and at the end of this field, in the left corner, go over another stile (very wobbly) and the path divides. Here we fork right and cross the next field towards the woods. The path leads us past the right end of the small pond.

Just a few yards to the left of the path is a small memorial to Spencer Comley (1911-1989) of Astley Estate (which was owned by the Vernon family, who also owned Hanbury Hall).

Walk through the woods climbing up the other side of the small valley, passing a rocky outcrop and remnants of an old building. Reach the lake, **Nutnell Pool**, and turn right along the dam.

To the right of here, down in the valley, is the site of a forge operated by Andrew Yarranton who created an iron works here in the mid 17th century. Iron cinders

were brought up the Severn and then up Dick Brook which was probably the first canalised brook in England. The iron works subsequently were used for tin plating and later for grinding flint, for the porcelain works in Worcester.

At the end of the dam turn right for about 30 yards and then left to climb up the field with the hedge on our right. At the top of the field, go through a gate out onto a track where we turn right. Follow this track to a T-junction where the left turn leads to the **monastery** which has been a Franciscan brotherhood and retreat since 1918. (1¾ miles)

The buildings, including the old clock tower, were the stable block of the grand house which was destroyed by fire in 1810.

② Retrace steps from the monastery to the T-junction and keep straight ahead along the track through fields, where skylarks can be heard, and this leads us down to the lodge houses and then the main B4196 road. **Shrawley** village is a ¼ mile to the right, but we turn left for a few yards, to cross over **Glazen Bridge** and then turn

THE NEW INN AT SHRAWLEY WOOD.

right along the driveway to **Woodend**.

On the bridge is an old, almost illegible, notice which tells us that the parapet walls of this bridge were destroyed by a great flood in September 1852. Another plaque gives the name, Glazen Bridge, dated 1925 when the old bridge was demolished.

After about 30 yards along the Woodend driveway, fork right over the cattle grid and walk across two small fields and onto a broad track. Conifers cover the slope to the left and the small river, **Dick Brook**, is to our right. Reach another gate and keep ahead into woodland with small trees and evidence of coppicing. The path is a broad track here as we walk down the valley. On the right is the location of an **old forge**, just before we reach the stepping stones. Snowdrops and daffodils, and later in the year bluebells and ramsons, grow near the stepping stones, and the stream is home to grey wagtails. (1¾ miles)

③ Keep straight ahead, passing the short path leading right to the stepping stones and, after 25 yards along the fenced track, turn left over the stile and climb up into the woods. At the top of the climb, turn right for about 20 yards and then left across the field, to pass alongside a wood to our right – carpeted with bluebells in the spring. Keep straight ahead across the open field and turn left a few yards to the stile. (You may hear skylarks again here.) Keep more or less straight ahead, with the path descending quite steeply down a shallow valley to continue across the flat lower half of the field to twin stiles and footbridge. Cross a small paddock and over a stile to reach the narrow road. Turn right for about 300 yards and then left along **Seedgreen Lane**, in the direction of **Larford**. Pass a footpath going left, and just beyond a house on the right, turn right following the footpath sign and staying close to the right margin of this field. Walk round to the far side, to the stile. From the stile descend the steps to the riverbank and turn right through a metal kissing gate to pass the static caravans and reach the **Hampstall Inn**. (1¼ miles)

This pub is very popular with boaters (as well as motorists and walkers), and has delightful riverside gardens and a children's play area. A good range of food and drink is available daily.

④ Walk along the road and follow it as it bends right, passing between houses. After about 150 yards, by the telephone box and just before the road turning to the right, we go left. Follow the track and, after passing farm buildings, keep ahead along a footpath. Woodland covers the land to the right and to the left is a wetland area. Soon reach an open field (where lady's smock grows profusely). Just before reaching **Dick Brook**, go on through a metal kissing gate, and across a small field to a gated footbridge. Several paths lead on from here, but we go left over a stile and then along the right side of a large field. The woods slope up to the right, and the river is across on the left edge of the field. As we reach the point where the river comes close to the woods and our path, go over the stile by a gate and continue straight ahead. After about 100 yards, just before reaching another gate, turn right over a stile and into the woods. (1½ miles)

⑤ The path divides but we take the right option, climbing steeply along a narrow path – and leaving the sunken track down to our left. As our path levels off, it widens to a fairly straight track. Pass a cross-paths by a memorial seat and two huge Wellingtonia trees. Wood anemones and bluebells are prolific around here in season. Keep straight ahead, passing another cross-path, as we continue along the broad track. After being joined by a path from the right, the track divides. We take the left fork, then walk along the margin of the woods, with open field to the left. This leads us through to a gate and the exit from the woods.

The information board tells us that the small leaf lime was dominant, but is now scarce. Shrawley Wood has quite a few specimens remaining, which is why 54 hectares of Shrawley Wood have been designated a Site of Special Scientific Interest.

A few yards along the lane beyond the gate, we walk between houses to reach the main road directly opposite the **New Inn**. (1¼ miles)

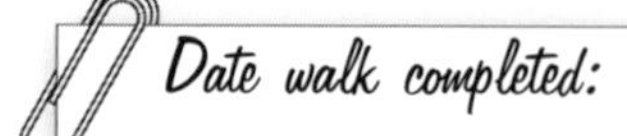

ABBERLEY HILL

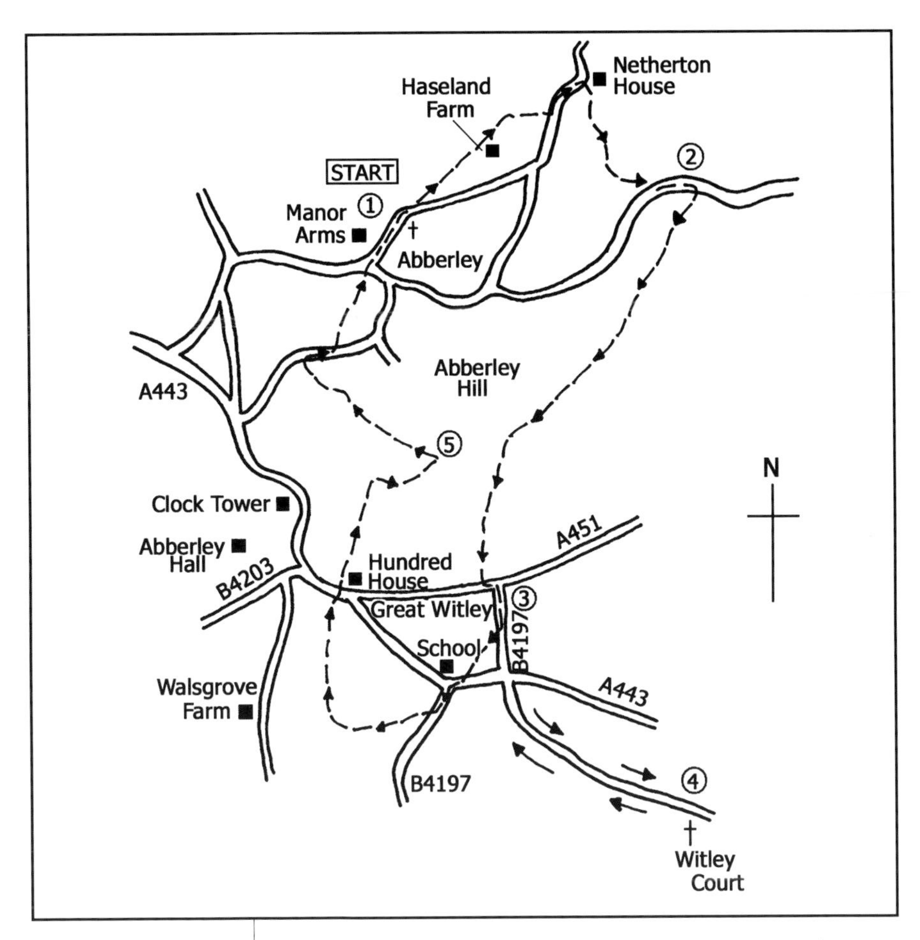

Distance:
9¾ miles (or 7¾ miles if not going to Witley Court)

Starting point:
The Manor Arms Inn. GR 753679

Maps: OS Explorer 204 Worcester and Droitwich; OS Landranger 150 Worcester and the Malverns

How to get there: *Follow the A443 north and then west from Worcester to Holt and Great Witley, then on towards Ludlow. Just beyond Great Witley fork right along the B4202 signed towards Abberley village, to reach the Manor Arms.*

THE 300-YEAR-OLD PUB AT THE START OF THE ROUTE.

The village of Abberley is situated in a hollow and surrounded by hills in the midst of wonderful scenery. The steeply wooded Abberley Hill overlooks the village and is a prominent feature of this walk. Passing through woods and across fields, we climb to the top of Abberley Hill twice and enjoy a succession of changing views in all directions. We also pass a goose farm. In addition to the two churches in Abberley, other outstanding local buildings are Abberley Hall which is now a school, and the dramatic ruins of Witley Court.

The Manor Arms at Abberley is over 300 years old, and was originally owned by the lord of the manor. The fireplace in the lounge bar is a particularly imposing feature, and log fires burn here in cold weather. Accommodation is available and walkers are welcome.

Good bar food, *as well as a tempting restaurant menu, is on offer, with home-made pies being a noted speciality. Real ales, and a selection of wines, will also enhance your visit. Telephone: 01299 896507.*

Opposite the pub is the Norman church of St Michael, which dates from 1160 and is a partial ruin, with a restored chancel. In the 1840s it was in such a state of disrepair that the new church of St Mary's was built, and its spire can be seen from the rear of the pub, as well as from several points on the walk. The day after St Mary's was dedicated in 1852, the tower of St Michael's fell down!

① From the **Manor Arms**, turn left along the narrow **Netherton Lane**, descending slightly and ignoring footpaths going off to the left. At the bottom of the slope, cross over the stream and immediately go left over the stile (signed 'Worcestershire Way and Circular Walk') and follow the stream and the left margin of the field. Up to our right is **Haseland Farm**. Leave the field over a stile and keep ahead along the driveway to pass to the left of **One Acre Cottage**. Proceed along the right margin of a field. Keep straight ahead close to the margin of a small wood and, beyond this, turn right over a stile. Stay near the wood at first but as our path descends, head over towards the left to reach a stile in the bottom corner of the field. Turn left along the road, as far as the first houses, where we turn right alongside **Netherton House**, to follow the bridleway, signed '**Worcestershire Way South**'. Descend at first, pass a small pool on our right, and then climb steadily along the track. At the narrow road turn left, with the woods and steep slope of **Abberley Hill** to our right. As the road bends round to the right, notice the steep ladder going up the hill on our right: this is our route ahead. (2 miles)

② A steep climb up **Shavers End** through the woods, leads us to the ridge top.

This delightful ancient woodland is rich in flowers and bird life, and occasional views open up across miles of undulating countryside, especially if walking in winter. A fence to our left guards the edge of the Shavers End quarries, famed for their limestone, but having ceased production in 1993 and now partially concealed by trees. Alongside the path are ancient yew trees.

The path levels off after half a mile in the woods and we are joined by the **Worcestershire Way**, which comes in from our left, having followed a gentler climb to the ridge top. About 300 yards beyond this junction of paths, we descend slightly to reach a cross path, (straight on is the Worcestershire Way, and there is a path to the right) where we turn left following the bridleway sign. After a mere 5 yards this splits with a path going left through the bracken, but we go right and follow this narrow route, rising slightly at first. Then we reach a level patch and a crossing point of four paths. We keep straight ahead here, along a compass bearing of 190° – more or less southwards. We soon begin to descend steeply, passing a wooden post with a yellow arrow and at the bottom of the wood turn right for a few yards to join a major track where we turn left. Carry on downhill in a sunken track between hedges. Keep straight ahead, passing between orchards, to reach the main road near the farm shop. Turn left along the A451 road and, after about 70 yards, cross over and turn right. (2½ miles)

③ Pass the modernised barn on the left, noticing the old barn door with a stone carving of a sheaf of corn above. After about 200 yards along this road, and just past the pool and stream on the right, is a time of decision. If you are planning to visit **Witley Court**, keep straight ahead along this road, to reach the A443. Go straight across here passing the **Lodge House** and follow the drive signed to **Witley** church. Walk along this drive for about a mile to reach the church and **Witley Court**.

Witley Court was one of England's greatest houses of the mid 19th century – a palatial mansion and the home of the Dudley family. Burnt down in 1937, it was then neglected until restoration work began in 1972. It is now in the care of English Heritage and open throughout the year. The dramatic ruined shell of the building has been repaired in order to make the walls safe, but the gardens (ideal for picnics, if required) are being restored to their former state, and woodland walks have been created. The largest of the fountains, Perseus and Andromeda, is in full working order. Telephone 01299 896656.

WALSGROVE FARM IS FAMOUS FOR ITS GEESE.

St Michael's church is on the site of an old medieval church, and was rebuilt by Lady Foley in 1735 (the Foley family having owned the estate before the Dudleys). It is a brick building faced with limestone, but the dull exterior gives no indication of the unforgettable interior, with painted walls and ceilings, and coloured glass. Near the altar is a memorial to the first Lord Foley.

After your visit, retrace your steps to the main road and turn left to continue the circuit. (Add 2 miles for this extension to Witley Court.)

If not going to Witley Court, turn right shortly beyond the pool, at the footpath sign pointing right, and head diagonally across the large field towards some buildings. Emerge on the road and turn right passing a surgery and the village school, and then go left along the B4197 towards **Martley**. Just beyond the first house on the right, turn right, to pass on the right side of a pond to a stile. Once over this, stay close to the left side of the field (with a stream and big barns to our left) to a double stile and along the left side of the next field. At the end of this, a path goes straight ahead, but we turn right, with the fence on our left and big barns beyond and possibly large numbers of geese, for which this farm (**Walsgrove Farm**) is famous. At the end of this field, cross through asparagus beds and straight on across another field to a stile and footbridge. Cross the next small field, to reach a gate and the main road, almost opposite the **Hundred House**.

Pause here for refreshment if required, as good bar meals are available. Hundred House dates from the 18th century and was the meeting place for the surrounding area. Stock sales took place in a neighbouring field, and a courtroom and cell were inside the building. These were used until 1872, when the local police station was built.

To the left of the **Hundred House**, follow the footpath sign pointing us away from the road, between the hotel buildings to our right and a house to the left. After a few yards walk into a field and turn right for about 20 yards, then left, to follow the old hedge field boundary as we begin to climb up the slope. At the end of the field go over a stile and keep ahead along the right margin of the field, towards the woods which cover the higher parts of **Abberley Hill**. Go over an old stile and follow the clear path in the woods, and keep climbing through the mixed deciduous woods, with an abundance of sweet chestnuts. The path divides and we go right, slightly downhill at first as we swing round the valley on our right. After a fairly level stretch, begin to climb again, diagonally up the hill. Woodpeckers, tits and nuthatches are numerous around here, as well as squirrels. Reach the top of the ridge, where we turn left along the **Worcestershire Way** again. (2 miles)

④ Follow the yellow arrow and the pear logo. We undulate a little but just follow the main path, passing a patch of holly trees, and paths leading off to right and left. Reach an iron fence on our left where views open up to **Abberley Tower** (built in 1883 by John Jones) and the school.

Abberley Hall School is set in 90 acres and has exceptional facilities. It is a co-educational boarding and day school for 8 to 13 year olds and has an adjacent pre-preparatory and nursery school for 2 to 7 year olds.

Then, after another descent and ascent, we reach the triangulation point (283 m), with its plaque saying 'Flagstaff Wood trig pillar, adopted and maintained by Bournville Walking Club 1994'. Descend to a stile and the narrow road, where we turn right and descend steadily. After about 200 yards along the road, go left down the wooden steps, following the signs for the **Worcestershire Way and Circular Way**. Descend very steeply through the wood to a stile and then turn left along the field margin. Good views to our right look across to **Netherton House** which we passed earlier – and the spire of the village church is ahead – to the west of the village. Pass over the next stile and go straight ahead to a stile just before the house on our left. Then cross the drive and go over two stiles and down to another stile in the bottom left corner. Beyond this is the driveway of **The Orchard**, which leads us into the centre of the village. Ahead is the Norman church of **St Michael** and on our left is the **Manor Arms**. (1¼ miles).

Date walk completed:

Walk 16

STOURPORT AND HARTLEBURY COMMON

A ROAD BRIDGE OVER THE ROUTE OF THE OLD RAILWAY LINE IN LEAPGATE COUNTRY PARK.

Distance:
7¾ miles

Starting point:
The edge of Hartlebury Common. GR 820705

Maps: OS Explorer 204 Worcester and Droitwich Spa and 218 Wyre Forest and Kidderminster; OS Landranger 138 Kidderminster and Wyre Forest

How to get there: *From the A449 Worcester to Kidderminster road, fork left along the A4025 towards Stourport. Less than one mile south of Stourport, make use of the free parking area alongside Hartlebury Common. An alternative is to continue on to town to a large car park (payment required) close to the Council building and the River Severn (GR 807713).*

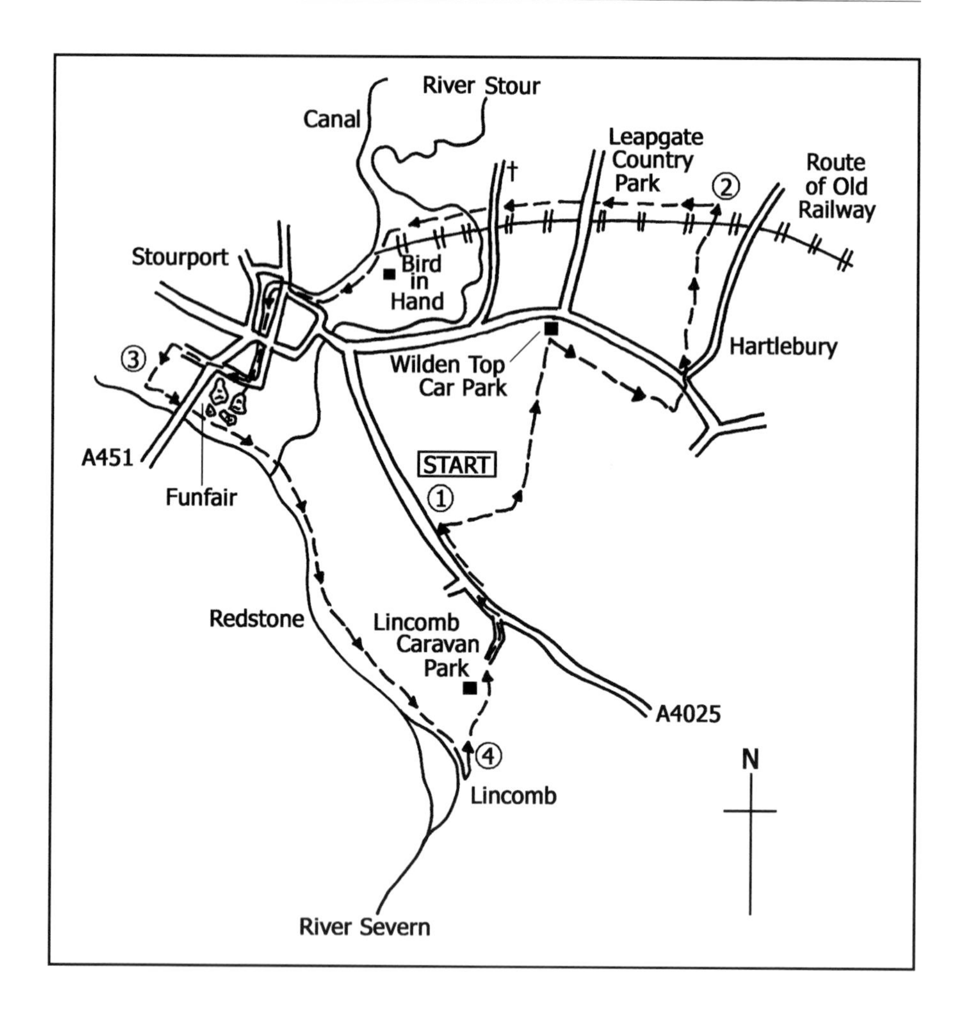

This walk will appeal to anyone with an interest in boats, canals and the history of a town which grew as a result of the digging of a canal. But it also goes past a funfair, riverside entertainments and across a heathland noted for its plants, animals and birds. We walk along the riverbank, on a canal towpath and along the route of an old railway which was developed to replace the canal and has now itself been replaced by roads.

The Bird in Hand dates from 1772 but has been extended in recent times. Former stables for the horses which pulled the barges have been converted into a comfortable bar and small restaurant, and there is a conservatory overlooking the canal, as well as open air canalside seating.

A choice of fine ales *as well as good food are on offer, and meals are served every day at lunchtime and in the evenings. Telephone: 01299 822385.*

① From the car park alongside the main road, walk onto the common in an easterly direction, and straight up to the top of the ridge.

Hartlebury Common is an 88-acre/ 36-hectare remnant of ancient lowland heath, now very rare in Britain. The geology of this area is mainly Bunter sandstone, and some Keuper, of New Red Sandstone age, but there are sands and gravels dating from glacial or postglacial times when large quantities of melt water deposited these sediments. Most of the heath is semi arid but there are a few boggy areas in the lowest parts, giving a wide range of habitats. The area was used for grazing in the past, gravel and sand was dug and there were rope walks here, as hemp was grown locally. Now it is the home of rabbits, many drought-resistant plants and is popular with nature lovers and dog walkers. This rather harsh environment supports lizards and grass snakes, but surprisingly there are no adders.

At the top of the climb, turn left and follow the broad and fairly level path through scattered trees, heather, gorse and bracken. Enjoy good views to right and left, with **Hartlebury** church tower just over a mile away to the right. Walking in a northerly direction along a horse route for half a mile, we pass to the right of a patch of conifers. Keep straight ahead at a major cross paths, to pass beneath power lines. When the track divides, take the right fork which leads to the **Wilden Top** car park. Here we turn right and walk along a stony track past the **triangulation point** (height 556 m.) and soon descend to a livery yard. Reach a T-junction, where a track leads right to a house. Turn right here for 20 yards, then go left through the hedge to continue descending to the bottom of the slope. Pass beneath power lines and then climb steeply up a flight of steps and go on across the level field at the top to walk to the right of houses. A path leads through a gate and a small coppice to a driveway where we turn left past the farm. At the road (the B4193), turn left for 20 yards and then right at **Charlton Lane**. Take the footpath between hedges, to the left of Charlton Lane. This leads through to large open fields. Go over the old railway bridge and then turn left to descend on to this disused railway line, now **Leapgate Country Park**. Used by cyclists and horse riders as well as walkers, this is a delightful tree-lined walk, rich in wild flowers and singing birds. (2¼ miles)

② Walk along the old railway line for more than a mile, often in a sandstone cutting, lined with trees and flowers. We pass beneath a bridge carrying a narrow road and then cross high over another road.

Just visible 250 yards to the right is All Saints' church in Wilden, famous for its wonderful Burne-Jones windows. Wilden was the location of the Baldwin family iron works and the church was built at their expense. Sir Edward Burne-Jones was the brother-in-law of Alfred Baldwin, whose son Stanley became prime minister.

THE BIRD IN HAND, ON THE BANKS OF THE CANAL.

Cross over the **River Stour** and over a narrow road near an area of recent building, and then leave the railway track to descend to reach the canal bank. Turn left here along the towpath to reach the **Bird in Hand** pub. Continue along the towpath and at bridge number 7, the Mitton chapel footbridge, a detour into the **Stourport** churchyard is possible, if desired.

A large and impressive building in Stourport was once the fine church of St Michael designed by Sir Gilbert Scott though not started until after his death in 1881. It replaced the earlier church of 1791, but work was never completed on the grand design which, in size and grandeur, was more like a cathedral than a church, and it was demolished after damage by storms in 1976. The small new and modern church is located on the site of the old Victorian Gothic church, a few remnants of which have been preserved.

Continue along the towpath. There are likely to be many boats tied up on both sides of the canal. At the **York Street lock**, there is Wallfield No.4 Bridge, an old lock keeper's cottage dated 1853, and also the **Lock Shop and Tea Room**. Notice the lock gates with the bent elbow shape, because of the lack of space for a longer arm. Here we come out on to the main road. Turn right, in the same direction as the traffic flow, to the main crossroads in the centre of **Stourport**. Keep straight ahead and then turn left into the large car park. Cross the grass to the river near the modern bandstand. (2½ miles)

③ Turn left to head downstream to the bridge, a graceful iron structure with stone pillars.

The first bridge across the Severn dates from 1775, and replaced the Redstone ferry. The present bridge dates from 1870. Near the bridge is the funfair, playground areas and boat hire firms – all contributing to make this a tourist town, the 'Blackpool' of the Severn Valley. Boat traffic on the Severn can reach up to about 200 yards above the bridge, but cannot go on up to Bewdley nowadays. Stourport is one of the very few towns in the world which owes its origins to a canal – the Staffordshire and Worcestershire canal. Stourport became a busy port, especially in the 1830s, but the Worcester-Birmingham canal which opened in 1815, and then the railways, brought about its decline.

Continue beneath the bridge, past the entrance to **Shipleys funfair**, where fairground music may help you get into your stride. Soon we reach a hump back bridge over the entrance to several basins, and the Staffordshire and Worcestershire Canal. Turn left just after this bridge to visit a flight of locks and then wander round the interesting buildings, boats and basins of this busy river and canal port.

The canal is 30 ft above the level of the Severn and linked by two sets of locks, one broad and one narrow. The larger are for the use of broader craft with a beam of between 7 ft and 15 ft. The basins are surrounded by fine old Georgian-style buildings, relics of the canal boom. The Tontine Hotel was built in 1788 and had a grand façade and entrance hall in order to impress the canal users. At the top end of the basin are two more locks, and some steps to a narrow road where we turn right to walk towards the Tontine Hotel (closed at present but hopefully soon to be restored). Turn right and walk down to the river with the Tontine on your left.

At the river, turn left to walk

downstream, to reach the bridge over the River Stour.

There used to be a power station here, opened officially by Earl Baldwin on 2nd June 1927.

The breakwater and the old warning sign about cross current still survive. Situated at the confluence of the Stour and the Severn, where the Severn provided ample water for cooling purposes, there was no need for cooling towers. It closed in 1984 and was then demolished.

Reach an open field, with modern houses across to our left, above flood level. Pass a short row of houses, with their own landing stages, and next we see the smart Severnside Caravan Park. Across the river are the cliffs of New Red Sandstone where a cave was inhabited by a hermit for a time, and also possibly by river pirates. On our left is a workshop area, a few old hulks of boats and, as we cross over the high footbridge, we can see the large basin with a fine collection of modern river cruisers.

The warning notice for the weir and lock is just ahead now. The **Lincomb** lock, the first of a series of six going downstream is under the management of British Waterways, Severn Navigation. The lock keeper's cottage is across to the right, and on our left now is a small wetland area. (2 miles)

④ Proceed downstream beyond the lock and, after 100 yards, use the footbridge to cross a small tributary stream. Here we leave the riverside path to turn sharp left. Now we are walking along the other side of the wetland, with a steep sandstone slope to our right. This slope is covered with wildflowers in spring, and the wetland is a wildlife haven for flowers and birds. The path leads through to an open area where we keep ahead passing close to the telegraph poles, and we walk on to a grassy play area in a caravan site. When we reach the tarmac surface, bend to the right to walk between the caravans and this will lead us through to the road.

From the entrance gates of the **Lincomb Caravan Site**, follow the narrow road, pass a line of poplars on the right and then the lovely red sandstone wall of a farm building, before the road splits and we take the left fork. At the main road we turn left along the pavement as far as the **Titton Stores**, and on beyond the turning to the Sandy Lane Industrial Estate and Marina, to soon cross over to our starting point on the edge of the common. (1 mile)

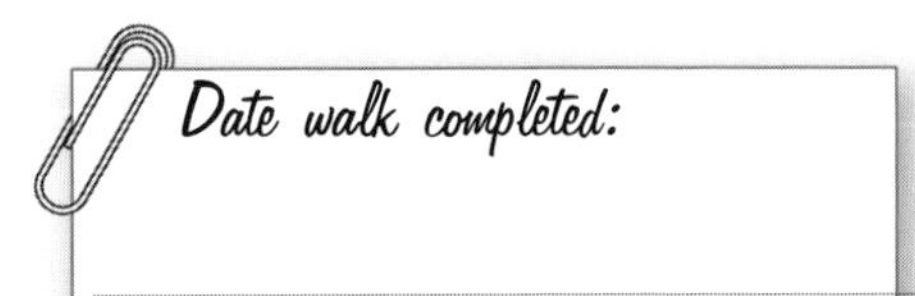

Walk 17

CHADDESLEY CORBETT AND HARVINGTON HALL

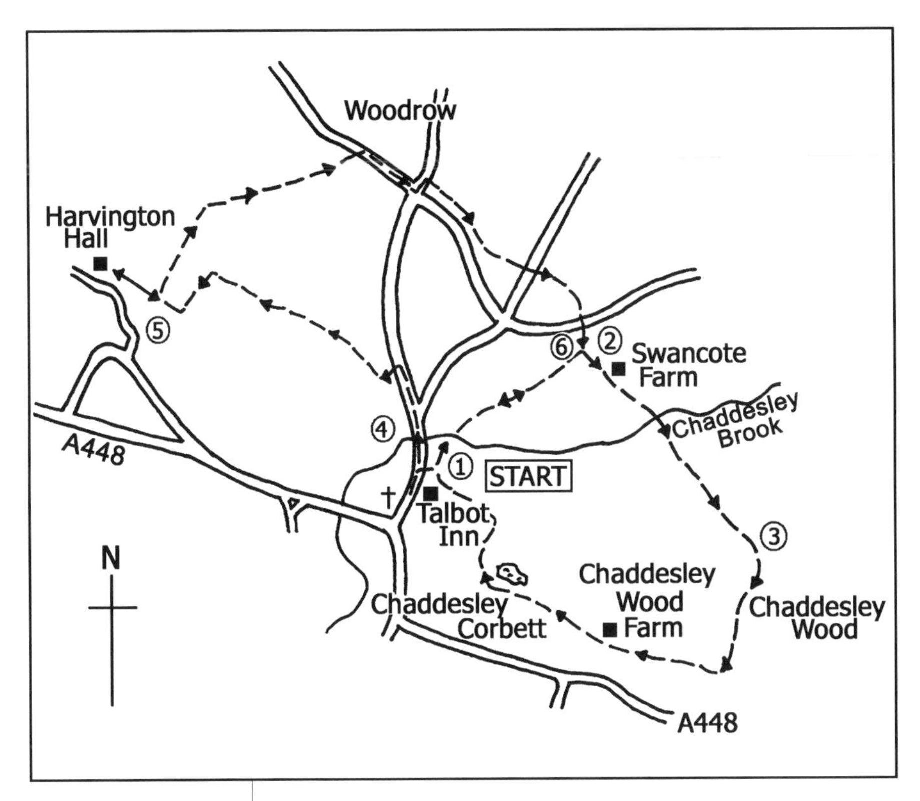

Distance:
10¼ miles, but with shorter options

Starting point:
The Talbot Inn at Chaddesley Corbett. GR 892736

Maps: OS Explorer 219 Wolverhampton and Dudley: OS Landranger 139 Birmingham and surrounding area

How to get there: *The A448 Kidderminster to Bromsgrove road passes within half a mile of Chaddesley Corbett, midway between the two towns. Turn onto the minor road into Chaddesley Corbett and park along the roadside near the church, or at the pub (with permission).*

HARVINGTON HALL.

The impressive sandstone church dedicated to St Cassian, a 4th-century bishop, makes an attractive starting point to our walk. The earliest parts of the church date from the 12th century, and amongst its outstanding features are the Norman arcades in the nave, a Norman font and the 18th-century spire. From the beautiful village of Chaddesley Corbett, we walk across the undulating farmed landscape, visit one of the county's largest and oldest woods, and also see Harvington Hall, which is noted for its wall paintings and priests' hiding holes.

The walk consists of two sections, to Chaddesley Woods and to Harvington Hall. These can be walked separately, in either order or as one continuous walk. The route is described to allow a break for lunch at the Talbot.

The Talbot Inn is an old black and white building dating from the 16th century – and there has been a pub on this site since the 15th century. There is a large car park and beer garden, with children's play area, situated at the rear. Indoors there is a pool table and a large bar and restaurant.

An excellent choice *of home-cooked food is on the menu, as well as specials on the board. Booking may be necessary at weekends. Telephone: 01562 777388.*

The Walk

① From the **Talbot** turn right along the village street and walk between very attractive houses, including brick and timber-framed structures dating from the 17th and 18th centuries. Opposite the **Swan** turn right along a lane and after about 60 yards turn left along the road between modern houses. As this road bends left, go right through a wooden gate and along the right side of the open grassy area. Cross the stiled footbridge and head across the middle of an open field to pass a few small pools. Continue along a narrow path, with a fence on the left and a hedge on the right – climbing slightly. The path then moves slightly right, up a few steps, and immediately left along the field margin, to reach a farm track. Turn right, towards **Swancote Farm**. (1 mile)

② The path heads between the buildings and continues along a grassy track between hedges. This leads us downhill along a track. Move slightly left through a small gate, but keep more or less straight ahead across the field, to reach the stream. Go on over the stiled footbridge and, after about 20 yards, reach a cross path. Keep straight ahead along the hedge passing to the left of a large pylon. Go through the metal kissing gate at the end of the field and along the margin of another field to enter the woods. (1 mile)

Chaddesley Corbett woods are managed by English Nature and the Worcestershire Wildlife Trust. Predominantly oak woodland but with some conifers, as well as an area of meadowland, this very ancient woodland covers 101 hectares. The acid soils support many wild flowers in the spring, notably bluebells. The wood is one of the largest managed by the Worcestershire Wildlife Trust and was part of the original, much larger, royal hunting forest of Feckenham.

③ The clear path through the woods climbs slightly and we reach a forest track but continue straight ahead for another 100 yards, passing conifers on our left, to reach a T-junction where we turn right. Join the forest track and, at a junction of paths, by a notice-board, fork left along a bridleway. This leads through to a gate and the edge of the woods. Continue straight ahead along the track for about 40 yards, then turn right over a wooden plank bridge to follow the narrow path between the woods on our right and a wire fence and open field to the left. Go on over a stile and along a narrow path between wire fences to another stile and then keep straight ahead across a large field, passing beneath the power lines again, and climbing steadily towards a mast at the top of the slope. Cross the driveway leading to **Chaddesley Wood Farm** and keep ahead along the left margin of the next field. Soon descend quite steeply to go over a stile and along the left side of the field, to another stile and along the left side of a pool. Once past the pool, go over the next stile and turn right to follow the field boundary.

We are now on the Monarch's Way, a 610-mile route following the escape of Charles II after the Battle of Worcester in 1651.

Soon turn left and then right, following the field boundary. Look out for a small stile, where we cross to the other side of the hedge, but continue ahead to reach the end of the field and a track, where we turn

THE TALBOT INN IN CHADDESLEY CORBETT.

left. As the track bends left, keep straight ahead over a stile and along the left margin of a field, and follow the path which leads us back to the main street through the village. The **Talbot** is to the left if lunch is required, but the ongoing walk is to the right. (2½ miles)

④ Turn right from the **Talbot** to walk through the village once again. On the right, just past the village shop and post office is a narrow road between a hairdresser's and a gift shop. However, we keep straight ahead along the main road to continue the walk to **Harvington**. Leave the village, cross over **Chaddesley Brook**, and after about 100 yards where the road divides, fork left. This narrow and sunken lane climbs slightly, but before reaching the top, turn left along a short track. The sign here mentions the Monarchs Way. After about 100 yards the path ahead leads into a field, but we turn right over the stile and cross the middle of an open field, close to the telegraph pole. Pass over the brow and as long views open up, begin to descend. Keep straight ahead through a gate, with a hedge on the right. Cross a stile on the right and immediately turn left to walk straight on, with the hedge now on the left. At the end of the field, go through a gap in the hedge and turn left, along a track. This soon turns right, with a hedge still on our left and, at the end of the field, tracks go ahead and to the left but we are turning right over the stile.

However, keep straight ahead if you wish to visit **Harvington Hall** which is only 400 yards distant. Continue ahead and bend left at the end of the next field, still following a track. This leads to a gate and straight ahead the road leads past the moat on the right and round to the main entrance. (2 miles)

Harvington Hall is a moated medieval and Elizabethan manor house, built in 1580 by Humphrey Pakington whose memorial can be seen in Chaddesley Corbett church. It was Pakington's family which probably created the hiding places for Roman Catholic priests. In 1696 the manor passed to the Throckmortons of Coughton Court, who owned it until 1923. It had decayed during the 19th century but was restored in the 20th century by the Roman Catholic Archdiocese of Birmingham. Wall paintings were discovered beneath whitewash in 1936. Harvington Hall Farm, with its large barn, is close by as is the Roman Catholic church which still serves a wide area.

⑤ After your visit, retrace your steps back to the stile and the route of the walk. Go over the stile and follow the right margin of a small field, and over another stile along the right margin of a young deciduous wood. We pass an old seat here, a possible location for a break or snack, if required. At the end of this field an arrow points us to the right. First pass the hedge on the right and then turn to follow the margin of the field. Reach a track and a small pond surrounded by trees. Pass to the right of this wood and follow the left margin of the field (or diagonally across the field if the footpath is clear). Reach a stile in the far hedge and continue diagonally right across the next field, or walk round the right margin. At the far right corner, a narrow footpath leads us through to a driveway and then to the road. Turn right to pass the delightful houses and gardens in the small hamlet of **Woodrow**. After about 400 yards turn left at the crossroads, signed towards **Hill Pool**, and once past the house on the right, go right over a stile. Follow the right margin of three fields and then take the narrow footpath between fences to reach the road (**Drayton Road**). Turn left here for about 20 yards and then go right over the stile. Follow the right margin of the field, with pylons and power line to the left. At the top of the slight climb, views open up ahead to **Chaddesley Woods** clothing the next hill. We descend and just beyond the pylon in the corner of the field, turn right and walk on to the road. Cross straight over and head along the driveway to **Swancote Farm**. (2¾ miles)

⑥ About 100 yards along here, turn right. A smart garden and bungalow is to our right and an open field on our left. Keep ahead, with good views to the church spire of St Cassian's, Abberley and Woodbury hills beyond. Pass the small pools to our right and then head straight across an open field in the direction of the church spire. Cross over the stiled footbridge, along the edge of a grassy garden, and straight ahead along the road. At the end of this road turn right, pass the old 16th-century **Malt House** with its stable doors, to walk to the hairdresser and gift shop on the village street. Turn left to return to the starting point. (1 mile)

Date walk completed:

Walk 18

LICKEY HILLS AND BITTELL RESERVOIRS

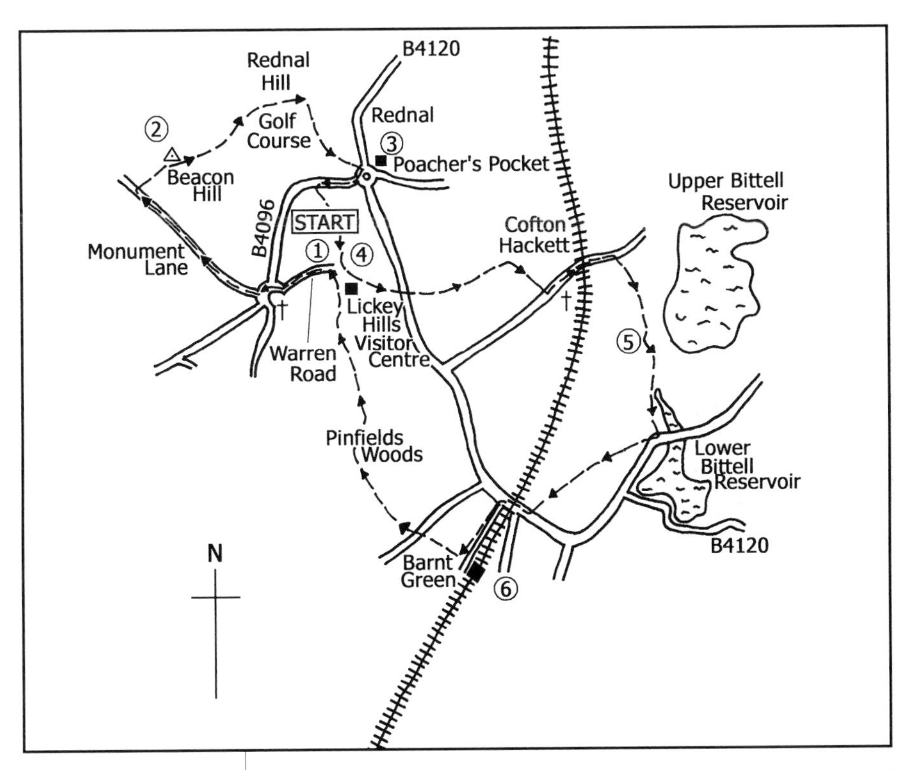

Distance:
8¼ miles

Starting point:
The Lickey Hills Visitor Centre, where there is ample parking. GR 998754

Maps: OS Landranger 139 Birmingham and surrounding area; and mostly on OS Explorer 220 Birmingham Walsall and Solihull, but Beacon Hill is on OS Explorer 219 Wolverhampton and Dudley

How to get there: *The B4096 forks off the A38, one mile north of Bromsgrove and leads into the well signed Lickey Hills Visitor Centre. If approaching from the north, along the A38 either through Rubery or through Northfield, take the B4120 towards Barnt Green, but turn right at the large island near the Poachers Pocket onto the B4096 to reach the Lickey Hills Visitor Centre.*

Up and down in the Lickey Hills and a lower walk across farmland near the two Bittell Reservoirs, gives a great variety of landscapes – and also different environments supporting a wide diversity of bird life. Crossbills and siskins visit the Lickeys in winter and the reservoirs attract a multitude of ducks and geese. The rocks of the Lickeys are amongst the oldest in England, with the 600-million-year-old quartzite forming Rednal and Bilberry Hills. The entire walk is close to the edge of Birmingham – but passes through rural landscapes, with views of Birmingham serving as a reminder that urban life is not far away.

The Poacher's Pocket is a large and popular pub, conveniently placed near the road junction in Rednal. It is open all day, every day, and there is an exciting play area for children.

It offers a good range *of food and drink to satisfy all tastes. Telephone: 0121 453 2795.*

The Lickey Hills stand at the south-western edge of the Birmingham conurbation, 10 miles from the city centre, and have provided a playground for locals for many years. The Lickey Country Park was designated in 1971 and covers an area of 524 acres (212 hectares). It consists of areas of deciduous woodland, coniferous trees, scrubby heathland and grassy patches. The Visitor Centre opened in 1990 (telephone 0121 4477106), and contains information displays and pamphlets, a snack bar, as well as toilets. Nearby are car parks, picnic areas and a children's playground.

① Start from the Visitor Centre and walk along **Warren Road** to the main road. Turn left past **Holy Trinity** church and then right along **Monument Lane**. Pass the Earl of Plymouth 1834 obelisk, a few yards to the left of the road, and continue along the road for about ½ mile to a large car park. Turn right here and cross the open grassy area to the mock castle at the top of **Beacon Hill** (978 ft/298 m). (1½ miles)

The toposcope on the castle

locates and names many of the features to be seen in the wonderful views all around, including Cannock Chase, the Malverns and the Cotswolds. A plaque tells us that this land was originally given to the City of Birmingham in 1907 by the Cadbury family. The toposcope dates from 1988, to mark the centenary of the parkland, as it was in 1888 that the Birmingham Society for the Preservation of Open Spaces purchased Rednal Hill and gave it to the city in trust.

② Walk straight on, in an easterly direction, passing to the right side of the mock castle. Come alongside the trees on our right, with grass to the left, and as we begin to descend, notice the **triangulation point** (938 ft/286 m) almost hidden in the bushes to our right. A clear path leads steeply downhill into the woods, along the line of the **North Worcestershire Path**, with its logo of a fir cone. The descent is aided by a line of wooden steps which take us down to a crosspath, where the North Worcestershire Path turns right. But we keep straight ahead along a narrow path, still descending, and then across a fairly level stretch to reach the edge of the woods. The valley bottom is on younger and softer rocks (Keele clay) than the steep hills, and part of this is used as a golf course.

The geology has influenced the shape of the land, but it is people who have determined the vegetation and the preservation of this country park area as an attractive scenic playground.

Go straight across the golf course. Beware of golf balls coming from the right on the first fairway we cross and then, on the second fairway, beware of balls coming from the left. Cross to the 16th tee, and then keep ahead along the margin of the wood following the line of the 15th fairway, at right angles to the two fairways just crossed. Near the 15th tee, go into the woods to the major track where we turn right for a few yards. Look for the path and old wooden steps going steeply up the hill and turn left here. Climb up through the bilberries to the path on the top of **Rednal Hill**. Turn right here to follow the clear path along the ridge, through bilberries with scattered silver birch and pine. As the ridge-top path begins to descend, keep straight ahead and drop steeply down to the road. Emerge close to the **Poacher's Pocket** near the island and the major crossroads. (1¼ miles)

③ From the traffic island turn right, along **Rose Hill**, the old Birmingham road to Bromsgrove. After about 300 yards, cross the road and go left following the sign to the **Lickey Hills Visitor Centre**.

This is just before reaching the Rose and Crown Hotel (0121 4533502) which was originally an old coaching inn on the old Birmingham road over the Lickeys. The road follows the steep valley known as Lickey Gorge, originally eroded by a small river but probably enlarged to its present depth by melt water during the Ice Age.

Cross the stream and the path immediately divides. Take the left fork up the staircase and climb steeply through the bilberries, with a few silver birch, pines and holly. At the top of the climb, we are on **Bilberry Hill**. Follow a broad stony path, still climbing slightly. As the path levels off, notice the dewponds to the left. Gradually we can see views opening up, first to the right and the obelisk, and then to the left, over Birmingham. Reach a viewpoint with diagrams naming features to be seen.

The dewponds are a relic of the time when this area was used as pasture. They were created by the Earls of Plymouth, who owned the land from the 16th century

THE POACHER'S POCKET IN REDNAL.

onwards, and they planted trees on land that had previously been dominated by bilberry, heather and gorse.

Keep straight on unless in need of the car or the visitor centre which are a few yards to our right.
(3/4 mile)

④ At the very end of the car parking space, where a large log blocks traffic from going further, we follow the **North Worcestershire Path** sign and fir cone logo. Walk along this broad path descending through the woods. At a major crosspath turn left, following the fir cone sign, to descend a stepped path to the B4120, Rednal to Barnt Green road. Cross straight over, towards **Cofton church**, and walk between houses to reach a wooden kissing gate and a large field. Stay near the left margin of the field, with houses to our left, the large field sloping down to our right and views of **Upper Bittell Reservoir** ahead. At the end of this field continue straight ahead. The North Worcestershire Path leads down the field and then bends right to reach the road, where we turn left. Pass the church of **St Michael and All Angels** at **Cofton Hackett**. There has been a church here since at least the 16th century though what we now see is mainly from 1861. Pass beneath the railway line, and when the road divides, the North Worcestershire Path goes straight on, but we turn right. A small stream is on our right, and then we reach a pond on the right where there might be coots, moorhens, ducks and even herons. The road turns left up to the sailing club and we keep straight ahead. The road deteriorates to a track, and it bends right and then left but, before continuing along this track, visit the reservoir by turning left over a stile with a very useful iron handle at the top.
(1 3/4 miles)

On the broad path, we pass the old pump house (which contained a steam engine made by Boulton, Watt and Co., used for pumping water up into Upper Bittell reservoir). The reservoir dates from the 1790s, being created as a feeder to the Worcester-Birmingham canal. Very popular with fishermen as well as boaters, this is also a popular place for ornithologists. Ducks (mallard, tufted duck, pochard and others), goosanders, geese, grebes and gulls enjoy the quiet life and the supplies of food in this lake.

⑤ We retrace our steps back over the stile and turn left to follow the track, between fields and **Mill Shrub**, a small pool fringed by reeds and bushes, and home to many birds. Walk on to reach a narrow road on a bend, where we turn right, over a stile.

Ahead and on the left is the willow-fringed Lower Bittell Reservoir (created to maintain water flow to the mills on the River Arrow, e.g. near Alvechurch) – and another location popular with ornithologists.

Follow the path diagonally left, passing a small clump of trees and a pond on our right. Reach a stile in the far corner and go over this and stay close to the field boundary. Then we go on over a stile and across a small stream and along the right side of a sports ground. Reach the road, alongside the Baptist church. Turn right here and once past the railway bridge turn left along **Fiery Hill Road**. Before turning left, you may notice straight ahead, the very smart and comfortable **Barnt Green Inn** which serves food every lunchtime and in the evenings (telephone 0121 445 4949). (1¼ miles)

⑥ When the station is on our left, we turn right past the large wooden gate and along the avenue of beech trees. The track leads us through to a narrow road where we turn left for about 10 yards and then go right following the bridleway sign. This broad path leads us through **Pinfields Woods**, with many ancient trees, including oak, hazel and birch. Carpets of bluebells and other wild flowers add colour here in the spring. The track climbs slightly and at a divide, take the right fork, and keep ahead, ignoring several minor paths. Descend to a small stream until the path splits and we bend left, still following the main track. Now we climb steadily, with the stream down to our left. A major track comes in from the right and here we see a signpost pointing ahead to the visitor centre. When this track divides again we take the right fork, signed to the visitor centre and car parks, and on our left is a more open patch of grass with an arboretum containing over 70 varieties of trees and a wooden sculpture 'The Spirit of the Woods' carved by Graham Jones, from an old sweet chestnut log. The visitor centre is now in sight, and we continue uphill passing the children's playground area to return to our starting point. (1¾ miles)

Date walk completed:

Walk 19

KINGSFORD COUNTRY PARK AND WOLVERLEY

THE OLD COURT HOUSE.

Distance:
8 miles

Starting point:
The large Blakeshall Lane car park at the north-east corner of Kingsford Country Park. GR 835821
An **alternative starting point** *is the car park in Wolverley village close to the Queens Head. GR 829794*

Maps: OS Landranger 138 Kidderminster and Wyre Forest: OS Explorer 218 Wyre Forest and Kidderminster; and also on OS Explorer 219 Wolverhampton and Dudley

How to get there: *Drive north from Kidderminster along the A442 towards Bridgnorth. One mile north of the town centre, at a small traffic island, turn right signed to Wolverley along the B4190. From Wolverley village take the narrow road (Blakeshall Lane) heading northwards and signed to Kingsford Country Park. This passes through the small settlement of Blakeshall to Blakeshall Lane car park at the north-east corner of Kingsford Country Park.*

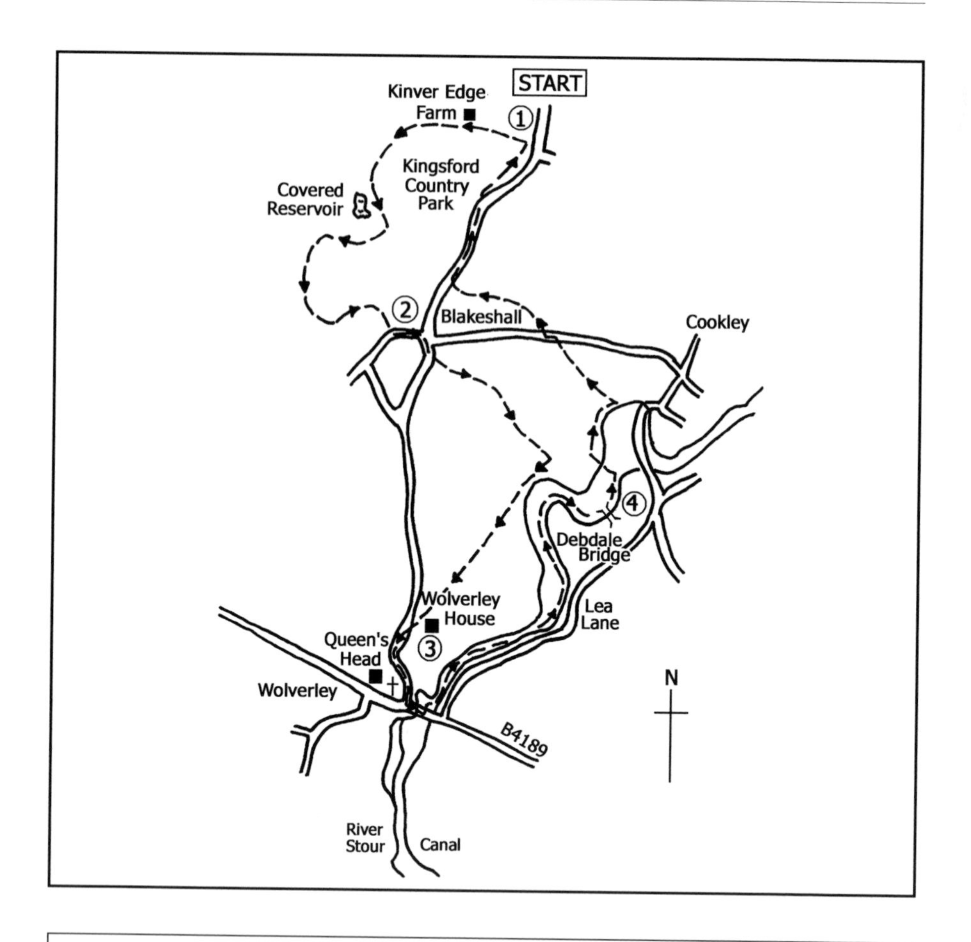

This walk from the woodlands of the Kingsford Country Park leads past Blakeshall and down through the deeply cut Stour Valley to the hidden and quiet village of Wolverley. It passes through a small sandstone gorge and moves on towards the imposing church, below which caves have been cut and several houses have been built into the soft sandstone rocks. The cave dwellings were used originally by workers at the time of the Industrial Revolution. From the village, the walk continues alongside the Worcester and Stafford canal before climbing across farmland to complete its circuit. Impressive views of the rural surroundings are to be seen throughout the walk.

The Queens Head in Wolverley is a popular family-run pub that sits in the centre of the village. There has been a pub on the site for over 400 years and it has an enviable view of the village church from its front door.

The good selection *of home-cooked food includes main meals such as ham, egg and chips, and a choice of baguettes. Telephone number: 01562 850433.*

The Walk

① From the entrance to the car park, follow the public bridleway sign and the **North Worcestershire Path**. Walk just inside the edge of the woods, parallel to a stony drive. The path is called a horse route and is sandy, ideal for horses – and not too bad for walkers, either. Once past the large house and garden of **Kinver Edge Farm**, reach a cross paths but continue straight on. At the top of a slight climb, reach an open grassy patch and another cross path. The **Staffordshire Way** leads off to the right, but we turn left.

*(Note: **The Worcestershire Way** formerly extended from here, but has been re-routed although some of the signs have not been removed. It now extends from Malvern only as far as Bewdley.)*

This is a very broad path, with a steep slope, the southern extension of **Kinver Edge**, down to the right. Occasional seats along here are placed to admire the views, looking westwards across glorious countryside. Pass to the left of a covered reservoir and begin to descend, then turn right following a yellow arrow and fir cone logo. After about 30 yards go left (where Blakeshall Severn Trent water sign is to the right). Turn right when a coppiced patch is seen on the left as we reach the edge of the woods. Pass a barrier to return immediately into the woods and begin to descend on a broad path. Bird life and bird song are likely to be evident all around – goldcrests, tits, jays and woodpeckers. At the bottom of this slope, reach a major path where we turn left. A road is soon visible down to the right. Climb slightly and then descend gently and as the broad bridle path levels, notice two turns to the left. First is a broad track going uphill, but we take the second, forking left on a narrow path, passing a few conifers and silver birch trees. At a major track, turn left and climb steadily. Soon bend to the right and continue up to the small lodge house of **Blakeshall House**, and reach a minor road. Turn left here and follow the narrow road as far as a T-junction. (2¼ miles)

② Turn right here, and proceed about 100 yards along the road towards the farm buildings. Go over the stile to pass to the left of the large barn and walk alongside the right margin of this long field. Pass over a stile and alongside the remnants of an old hedge, keeping straight ahead all the time. Descend to reach another stile and cross a small field to a further stile and continue along the dry valley. Shortly before reaching the next farm buildings, with a small pond to the left, go over another stile. Do not continue ahead towards the large metal gate, instead, turn sharp right along the field boundary, and climb steeply. Near the top of the slope move across to the left of the field as it levels off. A steep wooded slope descends down to the river. Stay on the edge of this field, and in the left corner reach a stile, beyond which we take a narrow path through trees. This is **Gloucester Coppice** – and like many other coppices was probably used for charcoal in local industries. The steep slope is to our left and an open field to our right. Leave this

THE QUEEN'S HEAD IN WOLVERLEY.

wood to enter another open field, with a fence on our left. Walk along the track, and soon reach a narrow surfaced road and pass between houses – with the drive to **Wolverley House** on the left. At the major road turn left and descend towards the village, passing the traffic lights and going through the sandstone gorge – called the **Holloway**. On our left are the buildings of the former Sebright School, including the Old Court House, opposite which is the **Queens Head**.
(1¾ miles)

The secluded village of Wolverley is set in the heart of a beautiful natural landscape in the Stour Valley, though surrounded by industrial towns. Dominant in the village is the imposing church of St John the Baptist, dating from 1772. Built of red brick on the hilltop, it is certainly commanding and contains many features of interest, including the large well cared for graveyard with several large tombs. The church is reached by steps and is definitely worth a detour.

Another outstanding feature of Wolverley was Sebright School, founded by local man, William Sebright. He became a very successful merchant in London, made a fortune and left it to the school which was endowed in 1620. It was closed in the 1980s, and the buildings are now used as houses.

③ Alongside the pub is the public parking area, close to several caves cut into the hillside, and the narrow road leading up to the church. This passes houses built into the rocks. From the pub, our onward route is to follow the main road as it bends slightly to the left, passing **Bishops Field Nature Reserve**. Cross over the river and at the major road (B4189) turn left (towards Stourbridge and Wolverhampton) for about 150 yards. Just before the **Lock Inn**, at the **Wolverley** lock, turn left along the canal towpath.

The Staffordshire and Worcestershire Canal is a James Brindley canal, opened in 1772 and linking the Severn at Stourport with the industrial area of the Black Country. It is a contour canal for much of its course but there are several locks.

The Lock Inn dates from about 1770 and has a large garden. Food is served all day Friday to Sunday and lunch times and evenings from Monday to Thursday. Telephone 01562 850581.

As we walk alongside the canal, the river is down to our left, and a rich wooded and wetland area is a major attraction for birds, flowers and butterflies. This is a very attractive stretch of rural countryside. Pass through a sandstone cutting, go on beneath a bridge and pass occasional houses and a wider stretch of canal. Just before **Debdale Bridge** and a lock, go left over a stile, with a signed public footpath to **Kingsford Forest Park** – the **Cookley Link**. (2 miles)

④ Cross the field towards the large factory buildings. Just before reaching the canal again, turn left along the track, with the factory on the right. Follow this track, across the river and, at the T-junction, turn right along a broad level track, with an impressive line of tall poplars to our right. After 400 yards look for the left turn signed to **Kingsford** and the **Cookley Link**. Climb steeply up the wooden steps, and come out at the top of the woods. Go on through the metal kissing gate, across the drive and straight ahead along the left margin of the first field and then across the middle of the second field to reach a smart wooden gate and the narrow road. Turn left for about 10 yards and then right along the bridleway signed to **Kingsford Forest Park**. This can be muddy and churned up as a result of horses, but leads us on between hedges for 350 yards. Reach a wooden post with a blue public bridleway sign and a symbol for the **Cookley to Forest Park Link**, where an old iron gate is to the right. Pass through this gate and walk along the left margin of the field, to reach a stile in the corner. Go over this and follow the right boundary of the next field to reach a stile by an old iron gate, and a crossing point of paths. We go straight ahead, across the broad **North Worcestershire Path**, and along the narrow track between hedges. Walk on through to a narrow road. At this, turn right and pass a few houses on the left, and then take the path on the left, continuing parallel with the road, just in the edge of the woods, to return to the car park. (2 miles)

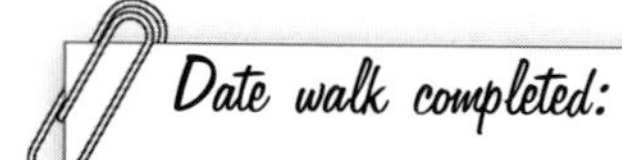

Walk 20

BEWDLEY TO ARLEY

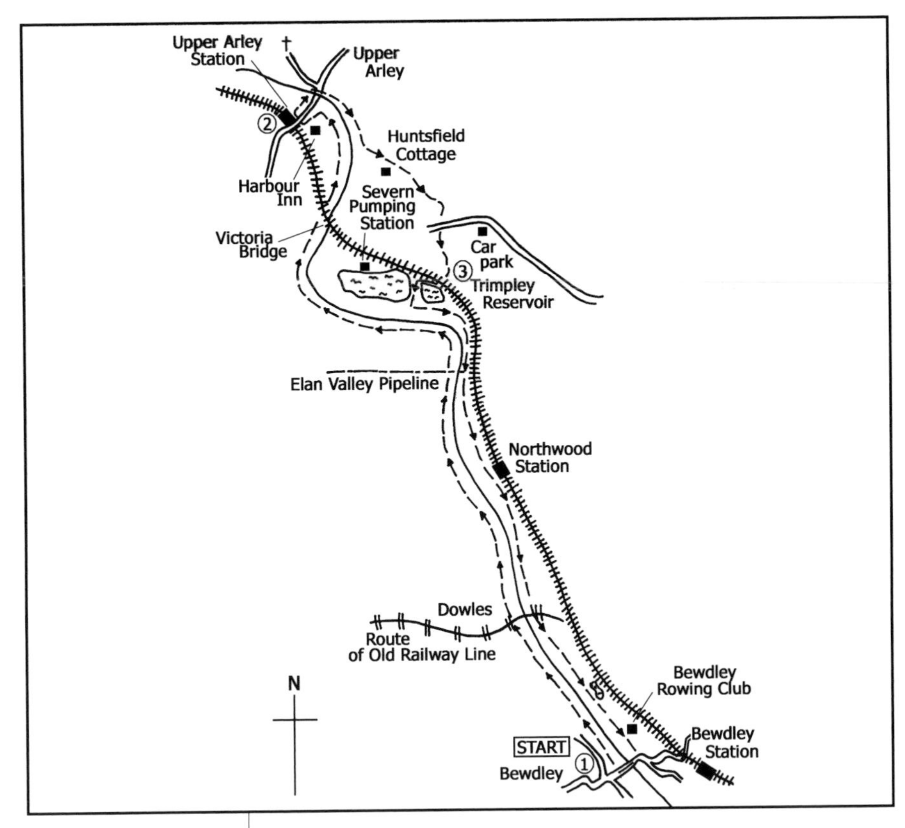

Distance:
9¼ miles

Starting point:
The main car park in Bewdley. GR 785755

Maps: OS Landranger 138 Kidderminster and Wyre Forest; OS Explorer 218 Wyre Forest and Kidderminster

How to get there: *Approaching Bewdley from the east from Kidderminster or Stourport, follow signs to the town centre. Cross the River Severn over the Telford bridge and continue along the main shopping street towards the church which stands in the middle of the road. Pass to the left of the church to reach a T-junction and turn right. After a few yards turn right along the B4194 and almost immediately turn right into a clearly signed car park.*

BEWDLEY BRIDGE, ONE OF FIVE BRIDGES PASSED ON THIS WALK.

This river valley walk includes woodland, five bridges and constant sightings of the river. There is also the sight and sound of the Severn Valley Railway (telephone 01299 403816), the famous steam railway which runs between Kidderminster and its headquarters in Bridgnorth. You may be tempted to travel one way on the train, and walk back alongside the river. The town of Bewdley contains many fine 17th and 18th-century houses, which was a wealthy period in Bewdley's history. Because of the river trade, many craft industries developed here – and evidence of the history can be seen in the museum in the Shambles, a late 18th-century market. Bewdley grew because of its river trade with Bristol and Gloucester downstream, and occasionally upstream to Ironbridge and even Shrewsbury.

The Harbour Inn is a very old pub dating from the 16th century. Nowadays it is popular with motorists and travellers on the railway as well as walkers. There is a garden area and a family room for children.

There is a choice *of beers and cider. Both sandwiches or full meals are available. Telephone: 01299 401204.*

The Walk

① From the Telford bridge of 1798, walk upstream, along **Severn Side North**, formerly Coles Quay. Pass a few houses, cafés and pubs including the **Mug House**. It was here that the bow hauliers, who pulled the boats upstream, waited for work. Across the river is Bewdley Rowing Club and on our left is a large car park.

From here, the Worcestershire Way goes south for 31 miles to Malvern but we are following the North Worcestershire Path. Note: The Worcestershire Way formerly went further north but has been re-routed, although all the old signs have not been removed.

Pass through a small park with some houses, followed by an area of caravans on the left.

Look out for birds – cormorants, moorhen, ducks, goosander on the river, and gulls overhead. Many land birds too, can be seen in the trees and woods which line this walk. The noise of bird song may be accompanied by the different noises of the steam engine and whistle of the Severn Valley Railway, on the other side of the river.

Go through a small metal kissing gate and see more caravans as we leave Bewdley behind. Cross over **Dowles Brook** and on beyond the supports for the second bridge which carried the old railway line, from Bewdley to Cleobury Mortimer and Tenbury Wells, passing through Wyre Forest.

Notice all the numbered posts for fishermen, descending from the 40s as we go north. The countryside is much more open now, but occasional houses will be passed on both banks, sometimes set back a little to be safe from flood water.

We reach a small settlement close to the bridge carrying the Elan Valley water to Birmingham, and here is a real graveyard of old machines. Continue on along the riverbank, through an open field and then into woods which come right down to the riverbank.

This is part of the much larger Wyre Forest, where pirates lurked. They waited to attack boats and boatmen as the bow hauliers

pulled the riverboats, called trows, upstream in the 16th-18th centuries. In those days the River Severn was a major route, comparable to the present day M5 and M6 roads, and linked Bristol with Gloucester, Worcester, Bewdley, and on upstream to Shrewsbury and even Welshpool – when water levels were adequate.

The river bends left here, passing a small island and a slightly turbulent stretch of river – but we continue upstream in the woods. Bird song and wild flowers will be a feature of this stretch in the spring and early summer. Pass a large house on the left and on the right is the embankment of the **Trimpley Reservoirs**. The river begins to bend round towards the right, and we reach a footbridge. Pass a house on the left, and go on through a small wooden gate to emerge into an open field – ahead is Victoria bridge (built at Coalbrookdale in 1861). Pass underneath the bridge and continue along the riverside path through three more fields to reach the Arley footbridge (the fifth bridge) and turn left along the road to walk to the **Harbour Inn**. It is worth walking on beyond the pub to visit the station – beautifully maintained and decorated with flowers, as well as a variety of memorabilia from the old railway days. (4¼ miles)

THE 16TH-CENTURY HARBOUR INN AT ARLEY.

② Our onward walk is across the footbridge, constructed by the council in 1964 to replace the chain ferry which had been in use for centuries but was dependent on the river current to allow the ferry to swing across to the other bank. The site of the ferry can be seen 100 yards upstream.

The main village of Upper Arley is on the other side of the river, and prominent on the hilltop is the red sandstone church. The estate belonged to the Lyttleton family of Hagley and they added to the church which dates from the 12th century. A famous 14th-century effigy in the north chapel is thought to be that of Walter de Balun who was killed in a tournament in 1270, on his wedding day.

Cross the footbridge, and a notice at the end of the bridge mentions the tea rooms and **Arley Arboretum** to our left – but we are turning right, along the **Severn Way** and the former route of the North Worcestershire Path.

Arley Arboretum, with a listed walled garden, was first planted in 1820 by Lord Montnorris. After a period of neglect it was acquired by Roger Turner in 1959. He restored the arboretum and the walled gardens, as well as improving and building houses in the village. When he died in 1999 the estate was left to the Charitable Trust which he had founded. Telephone 01299 861368 for opening times.

Turn right, along the fenced path which is slightly elevated above the river. We soon reach a small footbridge and immediately beyond this, we turn left along the **North Worcestershire Path** with its fir cone logo, leaving the Severn Way with its logo of the trow. Climb steadily into the woods, passing a renovated building which could have formerly been a mill on the small stream down to our left. Reach a track where we turn left, signed 'North Worcestershire Path and Eymore Wood car park'. Continue climbing and then go left over a stile (still signed'Worcestershire Way and Eymore Wood car park') and straight on across open fields. Walk on through two kissing gates and fields to reach the top of the climb. Pass to the left of a small house, and stay near the hedge with **Huntsfield Cottage** to our right. Reach a stile and a stony driveway where we turn left. Walk through part of **Eymore Wood**, descend to a small stream and then rise slightly to a major cross tracks. Turn right here to walk on to a gate and a road. The car park and picnic place is to the left, but we cross the road to a gate – ignoring the entrance to **Trimpley Reservoirs** on our right.

Follow the clear path descending through the woods, across an open grassy firebreak, and then fork right when the path divides, to descend to cross the railway line, with care, and reach the reservoirs. Turn right here alongside the smaller reservoir. Then turn left to walk on the embankment between the two reservoirs. (2 miles)

The larger reservoir on the right is used for sailing, but both lakes attract a variety of water birds including great-crested grebes. Trimpley Reservoir stores water pumped from the river. This began in 1967 to provide additional supplies for Birmingham.

③ Reach the steps which lead down to the river. Across on the other bank of the reservoir can be seen the house we passed earlier. We are now on the **Severn Way** again, following the trow logo, as we turn left along the riverbank, near the Severn Trent pumping station. Follow the riverside path round the large bend and pass a few summer chalets to reach a brick house and the bridge carrying the Elan Water pipes. Here we come onto a track and then a narrow surfaced road, with the railway line just a few yards to our left. Pass a series of chalets and more permanent looking houses which line the river, as we diverge from the riverbank for 3/4 mile. Pass the small station at **Northwood**, then a bright red telephone box and, at a house called **Bridewell** with a driveway on our right, turn right over a stile and walk along the right margin of the field. Once past the house we reach a stile, and are now back on the riverbank. Cross through a few small fields and then a much larger field as we walk downstream towards the old, ruined **Dowles bridge**. Pass the Water Board building, with the flood level marker posts, go through the metal kissing gate and continue to walk back into **Bewdley**. The small lake, where a pair of swans nest, is followed by an information board about animal and insect life in the pond, and then a playground area. Follow the riverbank until the **Bewdley Rowing Club** building requires us to move left for a few yards and then walk along the road to reach the **Telford bridge** over the river. Turn right here to return to the starting point. (3 miles)

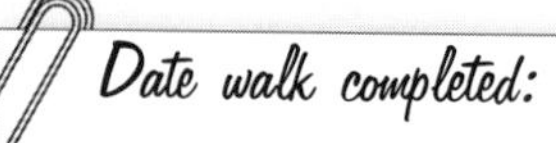